The Chicago River Architecture Tour

Phyllis J. Kozlowski, Ph.D.

First Edition

LAKE CLAREMONT PRESS

www.lakeclaremont.com
Chicago

The Chicago River Architecture Tour
Phyllis J. Kozlowski, Ph.D.

Published May 2008 by:

1026 W. Van Buren St., 2nd Floor
Chicago, Illinois 60607
lcp@lakeclaremont.com
www.lakeclaremont.com

Publisher's Cataloging-In-Publication Data
(Prepared by The Donohue Group, Inc.)

Kozlowski, Phyllis J.
The Chicago River architecture tour / by Phyllis J. Kozlowski.
—1st ed.

p. : ill. ; cm.

Includes index.
ISBN-13: 978-1-893121-33-1
ISBN-10: 1-893121-33-X

1. Architecture--Illinois--Chicago--History. 2. Architecture--
Illinois--Chicago--Guidebooks. 3. Chicago (Ill.)--Buildings,
structures, etc.--Guidebooks. 4. Chicago River (Ill.)--
Guidebooks. I. Title.

NA735.C4 K69 2008
720/.9773/11   2007940400

11 10 09 08   10 9 8 7 6 5 4 3 2 1

Table of Contents

Preface

All you need to do is go to any local bookstore and you can browse the shelves filled with books written about the city of Chicago. There are books on the city's history, her sports teams, her politics, her architecture, and even some of the unsavory people and events that have made headlines over the years. There are books without words that document the city and her people with dramatic photographs taken from the air and the water. So, why add yet another volume filled with words and pictures about Chicago to those already on the bookstore shelves?

Here's why. For the millions of people—Chicagoans and visitors alike—who come to the heart of the city each year, one of the highlights has been experiencing it from the Chicago River. On any weekend during the summer months, thousands of visitors line up to board one of the vessels designed to take them down the liquid highway that will provide unencumbered views of the spectacular architecture and skyline of a city rebuilt out of the ashes. The Great Chicago Fire of October 8, 1871, devastated most of the downtown area. Less than one week after the fire had subsided, the citizens of Chicago began to rebuild their city. Today, they are proud of what they have accomplished and relish sharing its architecture and history with the world.

Tour guides on board enthusiastically narrate the colorful history, architecture, and the metamorphosis of a city that once was referred to as the "hog butcher to the world" and is now competing for one of the most prestigious international prizes, the 2016 Summer Olympic Games.

This pocket-size book is intended to capture some of the highlights of your Chicago River Architecture Tour and to provide you with space to record your own comments. We hope you consider it a souvenir that is easy to pack and worth keeping.

Whether you have purchased your ticket in advance or are making your way to the ticket booth at Wendella, take a moment and stop on the Michigan Avenue bridge. One of the city's four double-decker bridges, it's an excellent place to see and experience Chicago firsthand.

The Michigan Avenue bridge with a Wendella boat in the foreground.

The bridge is always teeming with dozens of pedestrians, cars, and buses, but it's a perfect vantage point to see the river from above. First, look to the east and catch a glimpse of Lake Michigan and the Nicolas J. Melas Centennial Fountain with its water cannon activated every ten minutes on the hour during the late spring and summer. This area is experiencing massive residential development, partially as a result of an exodus from the suburbs and the desire to live along the river with a view of the lakefront.

View looking west from the Michigan Avenue bridge.

Now look to the west and you will see how this sleepy river once explored by a Jesuit priest and a French fur trader has provided a necklace to which architectural jewels have been added over the years. Notice the progress on the Trump International Hotel and Tower under construction, the distinctive circular towers of Marina City, and Mies van der Rohe's IBM Building, now known as 330 N. Wabash, an icon of the Modernist style.

Look to the right and you can see up close the detail on the magnificent white glazed terra cotta façade of the Wrigley Building, which anchored development north of the river and now, with the Tribune Tower, is the gateway to Michigan Avenue's Magnificent Mile.

I guarantee the experience will be rewarding. However, if you hear bells begin to ring and see lights begin to flash, be warned that the bridge is about to open. I suggest that you quickly exit towards the Wrigley Building or you will find yourself on the wrong side of the river for your tour.

The small plaza in front of the Wrigley Building is a gathering place for street artists and musicians, a popular stop for wedding parties to take photographs, and a great place to snap pictures of the river.

Michigan Avenue, home to Chicago's trendiest shopping, is filled with boutiques, designer shops, and major anchor stores. Shopping, however, will have to wait for now. Instead, make your way down the grand staircase to the Wendella boat dock.

There are several companies that provide boat tours on the river, but Wendella is the granddaddy of them all. A family-owned business now in its third generation, Wendella has been providing tours for thousands of Chicagoans and visitors since 1935. You will learn about the company's history later in the book.

Boarding has begun for your tour. For the best view, head for the upper deck. With camera in tow, you are now in a position to experience the city at its best.

Wendella Sightseeing:
A Dream Becomes Reality

In an age when corporate mergers and buyouts have all but eliminated family-owned businesses, Wendella Boats continues to thrive in its seventy-third year of providing locals and visitors with tours and taxi service on the Chicago River. The company's rise and premier status in the tour industry can be credited to three generations of Borgstroms investing in an American dream come true. Today, the company operates a fleet of vessels and employs more than 125 employees in a state-of-the-art operation that serves more than 100,000 guests during their operating season.

The company's roots can be attributed to Albert Borgstrom, a Swedish immigrant who left the family farm in Umea, Sweden, in the late 1920s to seek his fortune in America. His only experience with boats came from an apprenticeship he served in his homeland working as a deckhand on fishing boats. Like many immigrants, the reality of finding a job was not what he had imagined when he arrived in his new country. Eventually he found work in Wisconsin as a lumberjack.

After relocating to Chicago, he began working as a carpenter on boats at Navy Pier. At that time, most boats were built of wood, and a good carpenter could offer his services to a variety of shops located behind huge doors on the pier that provided access to the water. Albert, like other boat carpenters, worked for a variety of companies, including Gar Wood and Chris-Craft. His son Robert says that to supplement his income during the Prohibition period, his father, like so many others, made bathtub gin, which he sold and bottled.

Being an industrious person, Albert also enjoyed trying his hand at inventing. Although he never realized a patent for any of his ideas,

Albert (right, shaking hand), Michael (smaller boy), Steven (larger boy), Robert (man behind Steven).

he is credited with coming up with an idea for a pop-up toaster, the "wonder board," which massaged your feet while standing on it, and plans for a way to use heat from the earth to burn garbage.

Years of hard work, entrepreneurial investments, and careful budgeting resulted in the accumulation of a $7,000 nest egg. Finally, Albert could return to his native land with money for a fresh start. Unfortunately, as history would have it, the famous stock market crash of 1929 wiped out any hopes he had for going home and making a new start.

With no one to turn to for help, Captain Albert joined the U.S. Coast Guard in Chicago and was given an interesting rescue operations assignment requiring that he and his colleague sit in the two towers at Navy Pier and watch for shipments of illegal Canadian whiskey being brought in for one of the city's most infamous characters during prohibition, Al Capone.

The liquor would be brought in by boat and dropped off on the breakwall in anticipation of another boat picking it up. Captain Albert and his co-worker were to discourage this activity by shooting over the heads of the crew making the delivery, but never directly at them. Once the activity stopped, they were to gather the illegal cargo. It was not unusual for a case or two to disappear at the Coast Guard station before the liquor reached its final destination. The missing whiskey was lowered into the lake and brought up when the men's spirits needed a lift.

Early in the 1930s Captain Albert left the Coast Guard and returned to his original trade as a boat carpenter. It was while working on a yacht owned by an attorney that he got his start in the tour business. The boat, the *Wendela* (with one "l"; the second was added later), was severely damaged and had been brought in for repairs. Captain Albert and his partner offered to buy the yacht and to begin offering tours from the northeast corner of Navy Pier. His partner had already developed a steady business giving half-hour speedboat tours on Lake Michigan for ten cents. They agreed to start a one-hour tour on the *Wendela*, which had been gutted and outfitted as a tour boat. The 25-cent tour price would be split equally.

The original Wendela.

The business agreement ended when both men argued over how the speedboat revenue should be divided. They did agree, however, that Captain Albert, who bought the *Wendela*, would relocate to a dock at the base of the Wrigley Building and continue to give one-hour tours of the lake and river. His former partner would operate from the Navy Pier location. But keeping their agreement proved easier said than done.

An early shot of the Wendella dock.

Captain Albert's former partner, seeing the lucrative location, moved his speedboat operation directly across from the Wendela dock. The competition for business escalated and shouting matches often ended up in physical contact.

Captain Albert worked hard to make his fledgling operation a success. Tours were given seven days a week. The *Wendela* could hold 96 passengers, a captain, two deckhands, and a hostess/narrator. Business was good until one Sunday in 1941 when U.S. government officials arrived at the dock and asked that all passengers be refunded their money. The *Wendela* was confiscated by the United States Navy as a training vessel. It was a sign of the times, and all vessels commercial and private 65 feet or larger were enlisted to serve the war effort. Even the luxury yacht owned by Charles Walgreen, the drug-store tycoon, was confiscated. Painted grey, the *Wendela* proudly served her country without compensation for her owner.

Captain Albert once again saw his dream float away, and being too old for the draft, took a position working for the war effort building planes for Douglas Aircraft.

After the war, the *Wendela* returned home. The country was experiencing unprecedented economic growth and so was Wendella Boats. A new 42-foot vessel that could hold 40 passengers was added in 1948. The company became a natural fit for schools looking to provide a field trip, and boat tours up the river and around Goose Island were in demand. Today, the company serves hundreds of schools, especially during the late spring and early fall months, narrating the city's history and architectural legacy.

The *Wendela* was joined by several other vessels, including the *Sea King*, *Sea Queen*, *Queen of Andersonville*, and *P.T. Junior*, designed to look like one of the P.T. boats used during the war. The original *Wendela* unfortunately was retired when she was hit by an oil barge while docked at Michigan Avenue. Split in two and unable to be salvaged, she was stripped of her brass and other valuables and put out to sea. She was replaced by the *Sunliner*, which recently received a massive renovation and is now used as both a tour boat and for small charters.

Captain Albert had three sons. Although all the boys worked for the company at one time, it was Robert, his oldest, who would usher in the second generation. Just in case you're wondering, Captain Albert never retired. He continued to be a part of Wendella until his death at age 77. Now at the helm, Robert Borgstrom was to pilot the company's future. This was a time when the Chicago River rose from a stagnant polluted waterway lined with warehouses into one of the city's strongest assets.

As a family business, everyone worked at Wendella. Lila, Robert's wife, was cashier, bookkeeper, ticket seller, and jack of all trades. Their sons, Michael and Steve, worked as deckhands and ultimately received their captain's licenses. At times, they even narrated tours.

In 1962 Wendella started a rush-hour commuter service between Michigan Avenue and the Northwestern railroad station providing a unique, inexpensive, environmentally-friendly, and fast way to get from the train station to work. The service grew rapidly, and in 2001 the Chicago Transportation Study recommended the RiverBus, which the

The Wendella water taxi.

service came to be called, for inclusion in the federal government's Congestion Mitigation and Air Quality Improvement Program.

The program is aimed at reducing traffic congestion and improving air quality in urban areas. It also determined that the RiverBus provided a measurable benefit in reduction of auto emissions and auto congestion in the crowded downtown area and recognized it as Chicago's only viable water transportation system. Wendella was awarded federal funding for construction of a new vessel to expand the scope and frequency of the service. Today, the company operates the *Alpha* and the *Bravo* and is expanding the service to be called the Chicago Water Taxi. Plans are underway to expand the number of stops and to provide other conveniences on board for passengers choosing to use the service.

Robert continued to offer the company's mainstay, which was a one-and-a-half hour Lake and River Tour that is an original of the company and continues to be one of its most popular attractions.

As young men growing up on the river, Michael and Steve learned from Captain Albert and their father. "Dad was not always the most patient teacher," said Steve, the oldest of the two Borgstrom boys and now vice-president of the company. "I remember leaving the dock and my dad shouting commands in rapid-fire succession on how to back the boat out. I became so frustrated that I actually backed into the Wrigley Building. I think I moved the clock in its tower ahead 20 minutes. After agreeing it was the wrong way, we ended up at the famous Billy Goat Tavern, a favorite watering spot for everyone working on the river." Steve did get his license in 1974 and like his brother and their dad, all three of the Borgstroms maintain active captain's licenses.

When asked what some of their memories were of being young captains on the river, both responded that they remember the unique smell of sugar that came from the Curtiss Candy Company, which was located near North Pier (now River East). You could almost taste the Baby Ruths and Butterfingers as you went past the Ogden Slip. Of course, there was always the not-so-dainty smells that spread from the Union Stock Yards that operated until 1971. For years, the Yards dumped waste into the river creating what came to be known as "Bubbly Creek."

According to both Michael and Steve, there were fewer regulations and much more freedom on the river than there are today. Anyone could run a pleasure boat without a license. All the captains knew each other, and boat people were hired from all walks of life, which made for a colorful combination of personalities. There was no drug testing or background checks. If you could drive or tie up a boat, be civil to the customers, and pull an occasional bridge jumper out of the water, you were fine. "We hired everyone from cowboys, carnival workers, a Harvard physics professor, hippies, a priest, and a few debtors who hid in the engine room of our boat while collectors visited the docks," said Michael.

Today the rules have changed. Most captains have gone through extensive training and all must be licensed. They are drug- and alcohol-tested and go through background checks. It's not quite the same, but then neither is life on the river.

In 2003, Wendella, which now has a fleet of six vessels, added the M/V *Ouilmette*. This vessel, along with the M/V *Wendella Limited*, has open-air top decks ideal for giving the architectural tours that are growing in popularity. Today, Wendella offers 18 daily tours, both the one-hour Chicago River Architecture Tour, which is documented in this book, and the popular one-and-a-half-hour Lake and River Tour that goes through the Chicago lock out to Lake Michigan for a spectacular view and a narration of the major sites and history of the city.

With the arrival of the M/V *Ouilmette*, the company also entered the charter industry. Although tours remain their staple, the charter and Chicago Water Taxi services are expanding.

The company welcomed the M/V *Wendella* in 2007. Designed by nationally recognized Blount Boat Builders from Rhode Island, the vessel accommodates 330 passengers. It features a climate-controlled salon that comfortably seats 80 for a sit-down dinner, a promenade that affords spectacular views, and an upper deck reached by two grand staircases that entertains 240 passengers. With a full-service bar and handicap accessibility, the new *Wendella* is one of the premier vessels on the Chicago River.

In 2003 Robert turned over the helm of Wendella Boats, Inc., to his sons. Although he is still actively engaged in the company, Michael now serves as president and Steve as vice-president. Michael has been actively involved in the Passenger Vessel Association and will serve as its president beginning next year.

From left to right: Steven, Robert, and Michael.

The company has grown to over 100 employees and was selected as the official boat company for the Tall Ships Festival in 2006.

An integral part of the Chicago River's history, Wendella has served an estimated 14 million passengers on nearly 200,000 tours and charters in the last seven decades. The RiverBus, now known as the Chicago Water Taxi, has carried an estimated five million rail commuters since 1962 and more the one million passengers since 1999. The company continues to expand.

From its days of 25-cent boat rides, Wendella has grown to be one of the most respected companies in the industry. Captain Albert's dream is certainly now a reality.

Chicago History: A Timeline

1693 Jacques Marquette, a Jesuit priest, and Louis Joliet, a fur trader and explorer, are the first Europeans to visit the area. Asked by the officials of New France to follow the Mississippi to its ultimate destination, they abandon their plans and begin to paddle up the Illinois River, stopping at Kaskaskia (today known as Utica). The Native Americans are so taken with Marquette that they escort him and his tiny party over the Chicago portage to the Lake of Illinois, now known as Lake Michigan.

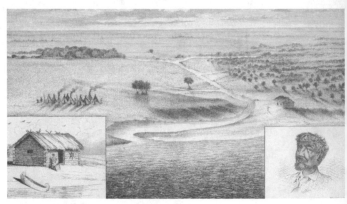

Chicago in 1779, with the cabin of Chicago's first settler, Jean Baptiste Pointe Du Sable.

1795 Treaty of Greenville is signed after the defeat at the Battle of Fallen Timbers in Ohio. Native Americans are forced to cede six miles of land around the opening of the Chicago River to the U.S. government.

1799 Jean Baptiste Pointe du Sable builds a trading post and establishes a permanent settlement on the Chicago River close to what is today the Equitable Building. He becomes the first non–Native American resident.

1803 Fort Dearborn is established on the banks of the Chicago River near present-day Michigan Avenue and Wacker Drive.

Old Fort Dearborn.

1812 Fort Dearborn is destroyed after Britain declares war on the United States. Military personnel and settlers leave for safety, but are attacked. The fort is burned.

1817 Fort Dearborn is rebuilt.

1825 Erie Canal is completed, giving easier access for immigrants to this new territory.

1833 Chicago is incorporated as a town and receives its name. Although we are not sure which tribe gave the name, we know that it is Native American and that it has a dual meaning. One meaning is "strong"; the other refers to wild onions that grew along the banks of the river.

1837 First drawbridge is built over the Chicago River at Dearborn Street. Chicago is incorporated as a city on March 4. William Butler Ogden becomes the city's first mayor.

1840 The first free schools and the first city hall are established.

William Butler Ogden, the first mayor of Chicago.

1848 The first railroad arrives in Chicago, the Galena & Chicago Union. The Illinois and Michigan Canal opens linking the Great Lakes and the Mississippi River.

1860 Cyrus McCormick establishes the first manufacturing plant for his McCormick reaper. Republican National Convention held in temporary building known as the Wigwam.

Abraham Lincoln nominated there as Republican candidate for president of the United States.

1865 Union Stock Yards open.

1871 Great Chicago Fire starts in a barn on the O'Leary property. 90,000 people are left homeless, 17,450 homes and buildings are destroyed, and 300 lives are lost.

The Great Chicago Fire ravishes Chicago's grain elevators.

1871 Montgomery Ward begins mail-order business.

1880 George M. Pullman builds his company town and opens his car shop to build Pullman sleeping cars.

1884 Home Insurance Building is completed. It is the first skyscraper, designed by William Le Baron Jenney. Haymarket riots take place as workers fight for an eight-hour work day.

1888 Frank Lloyd Wright joins the architecture firm of Adler & Sullivan.

1892 First elevated train runs between Congress Parkway and 39th Street.

1892 On May 1 the World's Columbian Exposition opens. Known as the "White City," it attracts 27 million visitors from around the world. Chief architect and planner for the fair is Daniel Burnham.

1900 After years of dealing with polluted water, the Sanitary and Ship Canal is completed, reversing the flow of the Chicago River.

1909 Daniel Burnham completes the 1909 Plan of Chicago.

1915 The *Eastland* capsizes on the Chicago River leaving more than 844 dead.

1916 Navy Pier opens for passenger and freight vessels.

The Administration Building and the Court of Honor from the 1893 Columbian Exposition.

1922 Competition for the Tribune Building is announced. More than 263 entries are received.

1927 Chicago's first municipal airport opens; it's known as Midway Airport today.

1932 Al Capone is arrested, tried, and convicted for tax evasion.

1933 A Century of Progress opens. Sally Rand makes her debut at the world's fair as a fan dancer.

1934 Bank robber John Dillinger is killed on July 22 outside of the Biograph Theater.

1938 Architect Mies van der Rohe arrives in Chicago.

1942 World's first controlled atomic reaction is achieved beneath the football stadium at the University of Chicago. Italian physicist Enrico Fermi is credited.

1953 Chicago is steel-producing capital of the world.

1955 Richard J. Daley elected mayor of Chicago. O'Hare International Airport opens.

The capsized Eastland.

1959 St. Lawrence Seaway opens, giving Chicago direct passage to the Atlantic Ocean via the seaway and the Great Lakes. Queen Elizabeth II and Prince Philip visit Chicago as part of the festivities.

1959 McCormick Place Convention Center opens.

1964 Beatles perform to a delirious crowd at the Chicago Amphitheater.

1967 Picasso sculpture at Daley Plaza is unveiled. Riverview Amusement Park closes.

1973 Sears Tower is completed.

1976 Mayor Richard J. Daley dies while serving a record sixth term in office.

1979 Jane Byrne is elected first woman mayor of Chicago. Pope John Paul II visits Chicago.

1983 Harold Washington is elected city's first black mayor.

1985 Chicago Bears win city's only Super Bowl championship.

1986 Mayor Harold Washington dies of a heart attack.

1987 Richard M. Daley is elected mayor.

1991 Chicago Bulls win Chicago's first NBA championship.

1992 Great Chicago Flood occurs when pylons driven to protect the Kinzie Street bridge rupture an underground tunnel system.

1996 Chicago Bulls win their fourth NBA championship and set NBA record for most season wins—72.

2003 Soldier Field reopens after major renovations. Meigs Field closes amidst controversy.

2004 Millennium Park opens and includes cover over the orchestra area by renowned architect Frank Gehry.

2005 Chicago White Sox win World Series.

2006 Marshall Field's department store renamed after being purchased by Macy's owners.

2007 Chicago Bears go to Super Bowl. Chicago puts in bid to host the 2016 summer Olympic Games. Mayor Richard M. Daley re-elected. 2000-foot, 150-story "Chicago Spire" by internationally recognized architect Santiago Calatrava approved by the city council; it will be tallest building in United States.

Architectural Styles

For years Chicago lived in the shadows of her raucous reputation as a harbor for gangsters and unsavory characters. Even though that era was short-lived, its stigma made it difficult for Chicagoans to point with pride to their city. Just as they were beginning to raise their heads, incidents such as the turbulence surrounding the Democratic National Convention of 1968 bent them back again.

Seventy-five years have passed since the likes of Al Capone celebrated Valentine's Day with a machine-gun massacre of rival gangsters and John Dillinger was killed by the FBI after being fingered by the Lady in Red. Chicago has hosted without incident the 1995 Democratic National Convention and many other great social and cultural events that have garnered her positive reputation of today.

One element of her esteem has always been the Great Fire of October 8, 1871, that destroyed more than four square miles of the city. Less than one week after the fire Chicagoans rose to the occasion, determined to rebuild their city. Although a catastrophic event that left 17,450 homes and businesses destroyed, 300 dead, and more than 90,000 homeless, the fire also had a positive side. It attracted talented young architects, including Louis Sullivan, John Wellburn Root, and William Le Baron Jenney, often called "the father of the skyscraper." Today, Chicago's architectural heritage has gained the city an international reputation.

Birth of the Chicago School of Architecture

Rapidly escalating land values in Chicago's central area motivated developers to build as high as they could. The invention of the elevator, flush toilet, indoor plumbing stack, and advances in wind-bracing and metal framing made it possible to go beyond the five-story limit before the fire. One of the most innovative ideas came with the introduction of fire-proofing a building using a cladding, or a second layer of terra-cotta. Cast-iron, which was used before the fire, melted under the intense heat. In 1871, the Bessemer process for rolling out steel was developed, and by the late nineteenth century became a staple for building the grid system for skyscrapers.

One of the main problems facing builders was how to address the weight of the new buildings. William Le Baron Jenney designed one of the first buildings to solve this problem by hanging the exterior walls on the steel structure. This innovative idea was the forerunner of what we call the "curtain wall" today.

The style of architecture that resulted from this new structural technology came to be known as the Chicago School of Architecture. It consisted of a masonry grid hung over a steel

The Home Insurance Building.

frame with large open spaces for maximum light and ventilation. One of the window designs that emerged was known as the "Chicago Window" and consisted of a large central pane of glass with two moveable sash windows on either side that could be opened. Excellent examples of these can be found on the Carson Pirie Scott department store designed by Louis Sullivan and on the lower floors of the Wrigley Building.

Another characteristic of the Chicago School was the three-part design consisting of an elaborate base or entryway, stacked floors, and a decorative cornice or top. Among the outstanding firms practicing during this time were Adler & Sullivan, Holabird & Roche, and Burnham and Root.

The World's Columbian Exposition

At the turn of the century, Chicago relished the idea of becoming an internationally recognized city and hosting the 1893 World's Columbian Exposition.

The Exposition, designed to celebrate the 400th anniversary of Columbus's discovery of America, would be awarded to the city that Congress felt could best host it.

Chicago sent her best politicians to lobby Congress and was handed the reputation of being the "Windy City," not for her wind velocity, but for the determination that her delegation were "windbags." The delegation was successful and in 1890 work began on a muddy site in Washington Park to create one of the most successful events ever to take place in the city. Known as "White City," the Exposition was under

The Administration Building.

the architectural guidance of Daniel Burnham.

The formal Beaux Arts style was deemed appropriate for this event, and the buildings were all built of a temporary material called staff. The only building that remains is the Palace of Fine Arts, which today is our Museum of Science and Industry. The Exposition brought millions of visitors to the city during its six-month run from May to November 1893.

Frank Lloyd Wright and the Prairie School

Chicago in the 1900s attracted another young architect of note, Frank Lloyd Wright. Although he did little commercial building in the city, he did develop a reputation and a school of architecture known as the Prairie School. This style complemented the flat prairie lands that surrounded Chicago. Using deep eaves and bands of casement windows, earth colors and open floor plans, Wright's Prairie style hugged the land. One of the best examples can be found on the campus of the University of Chicago. Built in 1909, Robie House is a national historic landmark and considered one of the best residential buildings designed by Wright.

Robie House by Frank Lloyd Wright.

Beaux Arts Style

The 1920s brought great prosperity to the city. With the completion of the Michigan Avenue bridge, Chicago also saw the beginning of a building boom on the north side of the river. The Beaux Arts style, finding a comfortable home during this period, centered around aesthetic principles associated with the École des Beaux Arts in France, an academy that dominated French architecture into the twentieth century. Many American architects were trained at the École or by other architects who had studied there. Among them were Louis Sullivan, H.H. Richardson, and Richard Morris Hunt. The academy emphasized the study of Greek and Roman structures, which these architects translated in American buildings, including many public structures such as train stations. Classical motifs, including decorative swags, medallions, urns, and elaborate ornamentation, were expressed on a large scale. The Wrigley Building is an excellent example of this style.

The Wrigley Building.

Just across Michigan Avenue, the Tribune Tower was built after an international design competition that drew more than 250 entries from architectural legends like Eero Saarinen and Walter Gropius. Col. Robert McCormick, Tribune founder, selected the winner himself. The nod was given to Hood & Howells from New York for their Neo-Gothic design.

Art Deco

Also popular at this time was a decorative style that came from the Exposition Internationale des Arts Decoratifs et Industriels Modernes that was held in Paris in 1925.

Known as Art Deco, it is characterized by strong verticals, the use of low-relief geometric shapes, stylized floral designs, parallel straight lines, zig-zags, chevrons, and the appearance of being machine-made.

The first Art Deco skyscraper was an adaptation of a second-place design for the Tribune competition. Located at 333 N. Michigan Avenue, it was designed by the firm of Holabird & Roche. Other notable buildings that demonstrate the Art Deco style are the Board of Trade by Holabird & Root and

333 N. Michigan Avenue.

the La Salle–Wacker Building by Graham, Anderson, Probst & White.

International Style

The Great Depression and World War II put a damper on building throughout the country and especially in Chicago. For the next 20 years few, if any, major buildings were built.

As the war escalated in Europe and with Nazi Germany looking unfavorably on contemporary design, architects and artists immigrated to the United States. Among them was architect Mies van der Rohe, who was head of the Bauhaus School in Dessau, Germany. Looking for a new director of architecture, the Armour Institute of Technology

The former IBM Building.

invited Mies to interview. He not only landed the job, but also was given the opportunity to redesign the campus of the Illinois Institute of Technology, which merged with Armour.

Concerned with structural design, he introduced the "glass box" to architecture. As Director of Architecture at IIT, he indoctrinated numerous young architects with his philosophy of "less is more." Many of the architects at Skidmore, Owings & Merrill, one of the principal firms in Chicago, have been trained under Mies. It was from this group that Bruce Graham emerged using his "bundled tube" structural system and the giant "X-bracing" that can be seen on the Sears Tower and the John Hancock Center.

The International style is based on modern structural principles and materials. Concrete, glass, and steel are preferred, and non-essential decoration is rejected. Ribbon windows and bands of glass give the buildings a strong vertical feeling.

Post-Modernism

By the 1980s, International-style buildings based on the grid and glass skin had multiplied so widely that they became the standard style for corporate headquarters across the country. Critics denounced their anonymity and hoped for a return to more passionate design. The response became Post-modernism, which brought back curvilinear and complex shapes, color, ornament, and historical touches like the dome, arch, and vault. What is clear about Post-modern architecture is its eclecticism, sometimes a jumble of ornamentation, styles, and historic forms.

333 W. Wacker.

Architects like Frank Gehry and Robert Venturi shone as Post-modern practictioners. Venturi actually attacked Mies's famous saying that "less is more" with his own version: "less is a bore."

Kohn, Pederson Fox Associates' 333 W. Wacker introduced a wedge of green glass to the cityscape; Adrian Smith of Skidmore, Owings & Merrill, resurrected Art Deco with his NBC Tower, and Thomas Beeby fused historical design in his Harold Washington Library.

The Chicago River Architecture Tour provides an opportunity to view all of the above styles. Architecture in Chicago is not static. It continues to excite the imagination and feed the ego. It has breathed life into the city and continues to do so.

Introduction to the Tour

There is nothing more exhilarating than sharing information about Chicago architecture with the thousands of Chicagoans and visitors who take our tours at Wendella. One of the things that the tour guides are constantly asked is, "Is there any place that I can get information on the buildings we have just seen?"

The answer is "yes"! This book is a synopsis of our tour, giving you an overview of most of the buildings we highlight. It is in no way intended to provide all of the information on each building, but instead, to showcase some of the distinctive features of each. Note that there is room for you to keep your own notes about the buildings! We hope you find our guide informative and that it serves as a reminder of the great number of architects who have left their mark on Chicago.

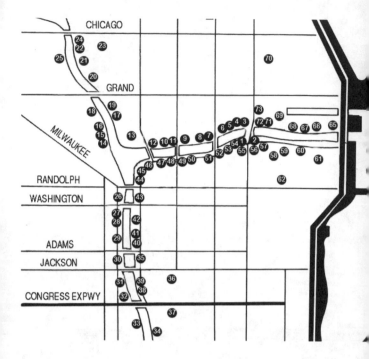

The Chicago River Architecture Tour

Points of Interest

63

31. **300 South Riverside Plaza**
Skidmore, Owings & Merrill, 1983
32. **Former Chicago Main Post Office**
Graham, Anderson, Probst & White,
1921, 1932
33. **Chicago Main Post Office**
Lester B. Knight Architects, Inc., 1996
34. **River City**
Bertrand Goldberg Assoc., 1986
35. **Sears Tower**
Skidmore, Owings & Merrill, 1974, 1985
36. **Chicago Board of Trade**
Holabird & Root, 1930 Murphy/Jahn;
Shaw Assoc.; Swanke, Hayden, Connell,
1980; Fujikawa, Johnson, 1997
37. **Chicago Stock Exchange**
Skidmore, Owings & Merrill, 1985
38. **Thermal Chicago Corporation Cooling Plant**
Eckenhoff Saunders, 1996
39. **311 South Wacker Drive**
Kohn, Pedersen & Fox, 1990
40. **200 South Wacker Drive**
Harry Weese & Assoc., 1981
41. **Chicago Mercantile Exchange**
Fujikawa, Johnson & Assoc., 1983, 1988
42. **Civic Opera Building**
Graham, Anderson, Probst & White, 1929
Skidmore, Owings & Merrill, 1996
43. **110 North Wacker Drive**
Graham, Anderson, Probst & White, 1961
44. **Great Lakes Building**
Holabird & Roche, 1912
Schipporeit, Inc., 1983
45. **191 North Wacker**
Kohn, Pedersen & Fox, 2002
Kendall/Heaton Assoc.
46. **333 W. Wacker Drive**
Kohn, Pedersen & Fox, 1983
Perkins & Will
47. **225 W. Wacker Drive**
Kohn, Pedersen & Fox, 1989
48. **222 North LaSalle**
Graham, Anderson, Probst & White,
1927
Skidmore, Owings & Merrill, 1986
49. **LaSalle-Wacker Building**
Holabird & Root; Rebori, Dewey,
Wentworth & McCormick, 1930
Site of the Eastland Disaster
50. **Waterview Tower**
Teng & Assoc. Scheduled for
Completion 2009
51. **77 West Wacker**
(United AirLines Headquarters)
Ricardo Bofill Arquitectura; DeStefano
& Partners, 1992

52. **Leo Burnett Building**
Kevin Roche/John Dinkeloo & Assoc.,
Shaw & Assoc., 1989
53. **35 East Wacker Drive**
(Former Jewelers Building) Glaver &
Dinkelberg; Thielbar & Fugard, Assoc.,
1926
54. **75 East Wacker Drive**
Herbert Hugh Riddle, 1928
55. **360 N. Michigan Ave.** 1923,1922
(Former London Guarantee Building)
Alfred Alschuler,
56. **333 N. Michigan Ave.**
Holabird & Root, 1928
57. **One Illinois Center** 1971
Office of Mies van der Rohe
Two Illinois Center 1973
Office of Mies van der Rohe
Three Illinois Center 1980
Fujikawa, Conterato, Lohan & Assoc.
58. **Two Prudential Plaza**
Loebl, Schlossman & Hackl, 1990
One Prudential Plaza
Naess & Murphy, 1955
59. **Hyatt Regency Chicago**
A. Epstein & Sons, 1974
60. **Swissotel Chicago**
Harry Weese Assoc., 1989
61. **Lakeshore East Development**
The Regatta DeStefano & Partners, 2004
The Shoreham Loewenberg, 2005
The Lancaster Loewenberg, 2006
The Aqua Jeanne Gang & Assoc.,
Scheduled for Completion 2009
62. **Aon Center** 1972
Edward Durrell Stone; Perkins & Will
63. **Navy Pier**
Charles S. Frost, 1916
V.O.A. & Assoc., 1995
64. **Lake Point Tower Condos**
George Schipporeit & John Heinrich
with Graham, Anderson, Probst &
White, 1968
65. **Site of Chicago Spire**
Santiago Calatrava, Scheduled for
completion 2010.
66. **RiverView I & II**
DeStefano & Partners, 2001 & 2006
67. **Nicholas J. Melas Centennial Fountain**
Lohan & Assoc., 1989
68. **Sheraton Chicago Hotel**
Solomon, Cordwell & Buenz & Assoc.,
1992
69. **NBC Tower**
Skidmore, Owings & Merrill, 1989
70. **John Hancock Center**
Skidmore, Owings & Merrill, 1969
71. **Gleacher Center (University of
Chicago Downtown Campus)**
Lohan Assoc., 1993
72. **Equitable Building**
Skidmore, Owings & Merrill, 1965
73. **Tribune Tower**
Howells & Hood, 1925

Fort Dearborn

Michigan Avenue bridge at Wacker Drive 1803, 1817

Before we leave the dock, look to your left. On the site of the Michigan Avenue bridgehouse at lower Wacker Drive stood Fort Dearborn. Following a confrontation in 1795, the white man's government forced the Potawatomi to cede huge chunks of land, including a six-square-mile plot at the mouth of the Chicago River.

Fort Dearborn was officially established in 1803 with Captain John Whistler placed in charge. He arrived from Fort Detroit with his young family and 67 men who built the fort. Named for General Henry Dearborn, the Secretary of War under President Thomas Jefferson, the fort consisted of two block houses (one facing southeast and one northwest), a stone powder magazine, separate officers quarters, and a covered sally port leading to the river that provided a safe escape and a route for securing water for the fort. The fort had stables and a garden and a sharpened stockade fence that surrounded it.

Fort Dearborn was evacuated during the War of 1812 against the British. Fleeing in vain for their lives, the 52 men, women, and children who occupied the fort were slain in what is now known as the Fort Dearborn Massacre. The fort was rebuilt in 1817 and remained open until it was abandoned permanently on May 10, 1837. The first red star on the flag of the City of Chicago represents Fort Dearborn. If you walk over the bridge to the southwest corner and look at the pavement, you will see the metal markers in the sidewalk that delineate the actual site of Fort Dearborn.

Notes

Michigan Avenue bridge

Chicago River at E. Wacker Drive
1920—Edward H. Bennett, architect

The Michigan Avenue bridge handles two levels of traffic and is one of Chicago's four double-deck, double-leaf trunnion bascule bridges. The others are the Lake Shore Drive bridge, the Wells Street bridge, and the Lake Street bridge. The 225-foot-long bridge was modeled after the Alexander III bridge in Paris. With this type of bridge the leaves divide, rotate around a trunnion pin, and return to their fixed positions upon closing.

Before it was built, Michigan Avenue dead-ended at the Chicago River. Traffic was forced to use an old iron bridge at Rush Street, which has since been demolished. The Rush Street bridge had a center stanchion, which required some fancy navigation by vessels, which often resulted in collisions. The new bridge could be opened and closed in less than a minute and was part of Burnham's 1909 Plan of Chicago.

Large sculpture reliefs portraying the Fort Dearborn Massacre; fur trader and settler John Kinzie; French explorers Marquette, Joliet, LaSalle, and Tonti; and the Great Chicago Fire of 1871 can be found on the bridge, along with the Chicago, State of Illinois and American flags.

The Chicago flag's memorable symbolism involves a top blue stripe representing Lake Michigan and the North Branch of the Chicago River; a bottom blue stripe representing the South Branch of the Chicago River and the Illinois & Michigan Canal; and three white stripes representing the land to the north, west, and south. The four red stars in the middle recall the four major events in Chicago history: the founding of Fort Dearborn, the Great Chicago Fire of 1871, the World's Columbian Exposition of 1893, and the Century of Progress Exposition of 1933.

Notes

Wrigley Building

400 and 410 N. Michigan Avenue

1919–1924—Graham, Anderson, Probst & White, architects

Located at the bend in the Chicago River and at the beginning of the Magnificent Mile, the Wrigley Building draws its inspiration from the White City of the 1893 Exposition; the Giralda Tower in Seville, Spain; and Cass Gilbert's 1913 Woolworth Building in New York City. The building was the first major skyscraper north of the Chicago River and the first air-conditioned building in the city. It also features the Chicago window.

The Wrigley Building is actually two separate structures; the south section is 32 stories with the tower, and the north structure is 21 stories. The center bay has a three-story arched entrance leading to a plaza designed in 1957 by Solomon, Cordwell, Buenz & Associates. The plaza, now undergoing major renovation as part of the Trump International Hotel and Tower development, will become a pedestrian-friendly walkway lavishly landscaped to attract pedestrians from Michigan Avenue through to Trump's Tower west of it.

The building has a four-sided clock with dials 20 feet in diameter. In 1931, a sky bridge was erected at the fourteenth floor to join two offices of the National Boulevard Bank. Some say that Wrigley, who owned the bank, did this to avoid being accused of then–illegal branch banking.

The Wrigley family accrued their fortune by first selling soap. When William Wrigley got the idea to include a piece of chewing gum in every soap package, the gum soon became more popular than the soap. The Wrigley family has also owned the Chicago Cubs baseball team, which plays at (where else?) Wrigley Field.

The site for the building was specifically chosen by William K. Wrigley Jr. so it would be visible when looking north down Michigan Avenue from the Loop. Fully illuminated at night, it is probably one of Chicago's best known landmarks.

Trump International Hotel and Tower

401 N. Wabash Avenue
Scheduled for completion, 2009—Skidmore, Owings &
Merrill, architects

This 92-story structure will feature 472 luxury condominiums, a
five-star hotel, health club and spa, several fine restaurants, and
indoor parking. When completed it will be the third tallest
building in the city. The curvilinear façade with a shimmering,
stainless steel and glass curtain wall features elegant setbacks.
The base of the building sits amidst a 1.2-acre park with access to
the Chicago River and north Michigan Avenue via the Wrigley
Building plaza.

Originally on this site was the Chicago Sun-Times Building, an
excellent example of the severe Modernist style popular in the
1950s with its poured concrete, glass blocks, and a brushed
aluminum exterior. The building was designed by the firm of
Naess & Murphy in 1957 and was torn down to make way for
Trump Tower. The *Sun-Times* newspaper now is located at and
has naming rights to the former Apparel Mart just west of the
Merchandise Mart.

Notes

330 N. Wabash Avenue

(formerly known as the IBM Building)

1971—Office of Mies van der Rohe, with C. F. Murphy Associates, architects

The former IBM Building was designed as a solid, harmoniously proportioned box whose exposed steel frame and tinted-glass curtain wall was a direct expression of the no-nonsense corporate office tower. Fifty-two stories tall, it features double-glazed windows, with a thermal break making two walls completely separate. It was deliberately set back to accommodate a below street-level railroad spur that served its neighbor, the former Sun-Times Building.

The building helped to popularize the so-called International style, which had become associated with the Bauhaus School and Mies van der Rohe. Mies died in 1969 before the building, his second tallest, was completed. In the lobby is a bronze bust of Mies by the Italian sculptor Marino Marini. Ironically, one of Mies's students, Bertrand Goldberg, completely rejected his style and designed a project that significantly opposed the International style of the IBM Building. That project, Marina City, is located just west of 330 N. Wabash.

Notes

Marina City

300 N. State Street
1964–1967—Bertrand Goldberg, architect

One of the first residential towers to be built on the Chicago River, Marina City was designed as a city within a city to attract middle-class workers and provide affordable housing in the downtown district. Consisting of two 60-story, poured-concrete towers built in 1964 and 1967 respectively, the complex originally included 40 stories with 900 apartments, 13 floors of parking, a skating rink, a health center, and retail space. The building was converted to condominiums in the late 1970s. Once advertised as "a place for 24-hour urban living," currently there is almost no retail in the building, though House of Blues, a couple restaurants, and a hotel share the property and plaza space.

The design of the building is unusual, with each floor attached to a central stem like petals on a flower; apartments are pie-shaped and attach to a central elevator core. The balconies that surround the towers are cantilevered in a repetitive pattern for maximum light. An excellent example of Goldberg's organic architecture, the enterprise reflects Goldberg's theory that "there are no right angles in nature."

Marina City was often thought of by the architect as the most photographed building in the world. It has been used as a backdrop for many Hollywood movies, including *The Blues Brothers* with John Belushi, and *The Hunter* starring Steve McQueen, in which a car was driven from the parking garage into the Chicago River. Recently, an insurance company duplicated that scene for one of their TV commercials. Although 40 years have passed since its construction, Marina City still has one of the most distinctive designs on the Chicago River.

Westin River North

320 N. Dearborn Street

1987—Helmuth, Obata & Kassabaum, architects

Originally built as the Hotel Nikko for Japan Air Lines, the hotel was sold in 1996 and is now home to the Westin River North. Its design contrasts a light masonry with dark trapezoidal bays. The hotel connects to the American Bar Association Tower by a block-long promenade along the river.

Notes

_____

_____

_____

_____

_____

_____

_____

_____

_____

_____

_____

American Bar Association Tower

321 N. Clark Street
1987—Skidmore, Owings & Merrill, architects

At the west end of the promenade connecting the Westin River North Hotel is the American Bar Association Tower. This 35-story metal and glass tower contains over one million square feet of office space. The building was designed by Bruce Graham (who also did the Sears Tower) in association with Diane Legge and Richard Tomlinson. A contemporary interpretation of the Modernist style, the building's exterior of blue and green glass reflects the color of the river. An elevator housed in a small structure at the lower level allows guests to descend to a restaurant located at the river and promenade level. The ABA also operates a law museum here.

Notes

_____

_____

_____

_____

_____

_____

_____

Reid Murdoch Center

(formerly City of Chicago central office building)

325 N. LaSalle Street

1914—George Nimmons, architect

2002 renovation—Daniel P. Coffey & Associates, architects

An excellent example of a typical Chicago warehouse, this is one of the last remaining on the main branch of the Chicago River. It is an eight-story steel and concrete building with terra cotta ornamentation at the top. The lion's head at the top was the logo for Monarch Foods, which occupied the building for several years.

The building was once symmetrical, but one of the bays was removed in 1926 to make way for the widening of LaSalle Street. At one time, railroad sheds for the Chicago and Northwestern Railroad were located to the north of the building to transport goods and to provide riverside docking facilities. In 1955 the building was adapted for use by the City of Chicago Central Office. You came here to pay traffic violations or to get the Denver boot removed from your car.

In 2002, the city relocated its offices, and the building was renovated for commercial use. The lower level has been leased to a major restaurant.

The architect, George Nimmons (1865–1947), was associated with the Prairie School and the building shows the influence of that style. Nimmons with William K. Fellows also worked on the design of the huge Sears Roebuck & Company complex on Chicago's West Side. It was the largest building commission ever received at that time and has since been demolished due to neighborhood rehabilitation.

325 N. Wells Street

(Former home of Helene Curtis Industries)

1912—L. Gustav Hallberg, architect
1984—Booth Hansen & Associates, architects

Built to be a coffee warehouse for Chase and Sanborn, this building is an excellent example of adaptive re-use. Having originally only about 168,000 square feet, a floor was added during renovation. The green glass rooftop penthouse housed a boardroom, executive offices, and meeting rooms for Helene Curtis Industries and was designed to look like a ship's prow. The company has since relocated, and new tenants now occupy the building, including a commercial office furniture manufacturer.

To eliminate cooling towers, river water is circulated through the coils in the basement as part of the air-conditioning system. When Helene Curtis occupied the building, a beauty shop was installed in the lobby overlooking the Chicago River so that visitors could see demonstrations of the company's products. A riverfront terrace is located at the lower level.

Notes

_____

_____

_____

_____

_____

300 N. LaSalle Street

Scheduled for completion, 2009—Pickard Chilton,
architects

This 60-story, 1.5-million-square-foot building has been pre-certified with a LEED (Leadership in Energy and Environmental Design) gold rating by the U.S. Green Building Council. Plans include using the river water for cooling rather than a traditional cooling tower for air-conditioning, and an "extensive green roof," with low-level plantings to help mitigate rain water run-off, trees, and places to sit. When completed in 2009, the development will have a half-acre park, an outdoor plaza, and waterfront café along the river, and building amenities like a three-level, 225-car parking garage, an upscale restaurant, a fitness center, a conference center, a bank, and a sundries shop. The façade of the building is being clad in articulated glass and stainless steel.

Notes

The Merchandise Mart of Chicago

North bank of the Chicago River between Wells and
Orleans streets
1923–31—Graham, Anderson, Probst & White,
architects

When it was completed, this 4.25-million-square-foot building
was the largest in the world and second only to the Pentagon in
size. It actually covers a five-acre site. Built by Marshall Field in
1931 to consolidate 14 wholesale warehouses, the Merchandise
Mart contains more than 500 showrooms and 14 miles of
corridors that display home and office furnishings, business
products, and giftware. The Art Deco building is framed in steel
and sheathed in Bedford limestone. A lobby mural painted by
Jules Guerin illustrates Burnham's 1909 Plan.

Built during the Great Depression, the building hit hard times
soon after it opened and was sold to Joseph P. Kennedy in 1945
whose family managed the building until it was sold in 1998. In
1991, the first two floors were converted into a retail mall by
Graham, Anderson, Probst & White, adding 85 shops and
restaurants.

In front of the Merchandise Mart on the riverside esplanade
are busts of American merchant princes, including Marshall Field,
Frank Woolworth, Edward Filene, Huntington Hartford, John
Wanamaker, Robert Wood, Montgomery Ward, and Julius
Rosenwald.

Notes

The Chicago Sun-Times building

(former Chicago Apparel Mart)

350 N. Orleans Street

1977—Skidmore, Owings & Merrill, architects

Originally designed to house showrooms for the apparel industry, the building was recently renovated to house the corporate offices of the *Chicago Sun-Times*. The *Sun-Times*, you may recall, had their corporate offices on the site now being developed as Trump International Hotel and Tower. Removal of a parking garage and the creation of a new entrance has given the building a much needed lift from its prior reputation as one of the city's dreariest buildings. Many windows were added during the recent renovation to the formerly windowless façade to take advantage of the location's natural light.

The top floors, 16 through 23, house the Holiday Inn Mart Plaza Hotel, with 525 rooms offering spectacular city views. The bridge connecting it and the Merchandise Mart was designed by architect Helmut Jahn. Today, the Sun-Times building also houses the Illinois Art Institute.

WOLF POINT

This is an historic site that once housed the first hotel built in Chicago, the Sauganash Hotel, owned by Mark Beaubien. The city's name, Chicago, was probably selected at a meeting at the Sauganash by the city fathers. The word comes from the language of the Miami and Illinois tribes and means "striped skunk."

It was also applied to an onion plant that grew along the banks of the Chicago River and gave off a rather unpleasant smell. It has another meaning, which is "strong." Most Chicagoans prefer this one.

The Residences at Riverbend

333 N.Canal Street
2002—De Stefano and Partners, architects

This residential building's design pays homage to the bend in the Chicago River. Intent on providing spectacular eastern views of the main branch for all the units, the corridors are located on the west side of the building.

Because the building is so narrow, a traditional ramp to the parking garage was not practical, so homeowners with parking spaces are given access to a car elevator that takes them to the parking floors. The development has both condominiums and a limited number of townhouses.

KINZIE STREET BRIDGE

This is the site of the April 1992 Great Chicago Flood, during which newly installed bridge pilings ruptured a freight tunnel that collapsed, sending river water to flood most buildings in the central Loop area. After many unsuccessful attempts, the problem was finally solved by pouring liquid concrete that cured underwater. Though much of it was underground and unseen, the damage was extensive.

Notes

Fulton House

345 N. Canal Street
1908—Frank D. Abbott, architect
1982—Harry Weese and Associates, architects

This former 16-story, cold-storage warehouse, which stands between the train tracks and the Chicago River, was insulated with cork over horse hair. In 1979, architect Harry Weese began renovation only to be confronted with numerous problems, among them creating 500 windows in walls that ranged from 12 to 16 inches in thickness and removing 500 semi-trailers of horse hair and cork. When completed, the building housed 104 loft-style condominiums and 20,000 square feet of commercial space. The building sports a nautical theme with its round windows at the top reminiscent of ship portholes and the starfish exterior decorations that indicate where the reinforcement rods for the building are located. Fulton House is one of the few residential buildings on the river with its own boat dock.

Notes

_____

_____

_____

_____

_____

_____

Chicago River Cottages

357–65 N. Canal Street

1988—Harry Weese and Associates, architects

Located at the site of the terminal of the first railroad to reach Chicago, the Galena & Chicago Union, these five- and six-level townhouses, with 2,200 to 4,200 square feet of floor space, rate a second glance. Their exteriors are stucco framed with steel, and units have concrete deck floors.

Harry Weese, who was an accomplished sailor, endowed these townhouses with a nautical theme. The walls look like schooner sails; portholes and decks illustrate their location on the water. Each of the four townhouses has its own elevator to connect the various levels. These townhouses are unique among Chicago's housing stock.

Notes

East Bank Club

500 N. Kingsbury Street
1979—Ezra Gordon and Jack M. Levin Associates,
architects

This is a private health club and tennis facility built when a face on the Chicago River merited no consideration by architects. Today the building's owners have added vines and shrubbery to make its exterior more visually attractive, especially to their new neighbors across the water at Kinzie Park. A new apartment complex, Kingsbury Plaza, was completed on land to the north of the East Bank Club in 2007.

Notes

Kinzie Park

501 N. Clinton Street

2001—Pappageorge/Haymes, architects

2002—Nagle Hartray Danker Kagan McKay, architects

Kinzie Park is a relatively new gated community built along the north branch of the Chicago River. It features 70 four-story, red-brick townhouses, reminiscent of European row houses, with balconies and rooftop terraces, on property lushly landscaped with sculptures and fountains. The complex demonstrates the powerful draw of the river and near-Loop locations for recent home buyers. So appealing was this development in the marketplace that most of the units were sold before construction began. The high-rise tower to the north of the townhouses distinguishes itself by maximizing views by tucking the balconies behind the curves and angles of the building.

Notes

_____

_____

_____

_____

_____

_____

Kingsbury Plaza

520 N. Kingsbury Street

2007—Solomon, Cordwell, Buenz, & Associates, architects

The 47-floor, high-rise building consists of 420 rental units and an amenities floor that includes an outdoor swimming pool, a fitness center, a party room, and an 8th-floor rooftop garden terrace. Plush landscaping and a fountain decorate the entrance rotunda. The building connects to an existing promenade on the river that runs alongside the East Bank Club.

Notes

River Bank Lofts

(formerly Wallace Computer Services Company)

444–456 W. Grand Avenue

1909—Nimmons & Fellows, architects

Another excellent example of adaptive re-use, this building first housed a printing company. Designed by the same architects who did the Reid Murdoch Center, the building was constructed of heavy reinforced concrete with brick sheathing. The balconies were added to the lofts providing excellent views of the river for units on the west side.

ERIE PARK

This dog-friendly public park sits on a four-acre site originally scheduled for a 42-story condominium tower. Concerned about density, the city purchased the land and created a green space to serve the residents of several condominium buildings recently built in the area. A sea wall was added, and a former one-acre Montgomery Ward employee park was included in the plan. There is access to a river-watch area adorned with a mosaic by Chicago artist Ginnie Sykes depicting Chicago bridges.

Notes

Erie on the Park

510 W. Erie Street

2002—Lucien Lagrange Architects

Both Erie on the Park and Kingsbury on the Park are suggestive of European industrial design. The exposed cross-bracing steel structure and terrace setbacks offer interesting views on all sides. They offer a welcome change from more traditional condominium designs.

Notes

_____

_____

_____

_____

_____

_____

_____

_____

_____

_____

_____

One River Place

(former Montgomery Ward office building)

758 N. Larrabee Street

1930—William H. McCauley, architect

An eight-story extension added on to the vast Montgomery Ward complex, One River Place is connected to the original structure by an underground tunnel running beneath Chicago Avenue. The building features a four-story ziggurat tower with a sculpture, "Progress Lighting the World Through Commerce," by Charles J. Mulligan. After the catalog company failed financially in the late 1990s, its offices were converted into condominiums with a contemporary Art Deco theme.

Notes

_____

_____

_____

_____

_____

_____

_____

_____

The Montgomery

(former Montgomery Ward corporate headquarters)

500 W. Superior Street

1974—Minoru Yamasaki & Assoc., architects

2004—Skidmore, Owings & Merrill;
Pappageorge/Haymes, architects

This high-rise office building, recently turned into condominiums and anointed "The Montgomery," was once the address of Montgomery Ward's corporate headquarters. It does not have corner windows in keeping with the philosophy of Montgomery Ward that there will be no corner offices to give increased status to employees. The conversion replaced smoked-glass windows with blue ones.

Notes

_____

_____

_____

_____

_____

_____

_____

The Domain

(former Montgomery Ward warehouse and offices)

900 N. Kingsbury Street
1906–1908—Schmidt, Garden & Martin, architects
2002 conversion—Pappageorge/Haymes Ltd.,
architects

When first erected, this was the largest reinforced concrete building in existence. It was located along the river to take advantage of both rail and river transportation. At 1.2 million square feet of space, the enormity of the building attests to Chicago's once long-standing importance as a catalog sales center. It is said that employees used to roller skate through the warehouse to fill customer orders. The building's design follows the river edge, and its decorative motifs are reminiscent of the Prairie School of architecture. Like One River Place, The Domain has a newly added promenade featuring restaurants and boutique shops.

GOOSE ISLAND

Goose Island was created when Mayor William Butler Ogden, the first mayor of Chicago, began an excavation quarry for clay for bricks. The island remains commercial even though there was discussion about developing residential units on it. Its name is associated with the wild geese that used to forage on the island in the early years of the city. Kendall College recently moved to the island.

Notes

Chicago Tribune Freedom Center

777 W. Chicago Avenue

1981—Skidmore, Owings & Merrill, architects

A high-tech production and circulation facility for the *Chicago Tribune*, the Freedom Center contains ten Goss Metroliner presses, each on its own foundation; paper rolls are delivered to the presses by a computer-controlled railroad; and plates are made from microwave impulses. The facility can turn out more than 70,000 copies of the daily newspaper per hour. This building received the dubious honor of being named "one of the ten least attractive buildings in the city" in the *Chicago Tribune* itself.

Notes

100 North Riverside Plaza

(Boeing headquarters)

100 N. Riverside Plaza

1990—Perkins and Will, architects

A 36-story building, 100 N. Riverside was built on a difficult site bounded by the Chicago River on the east and over the Metra commuter railroad line. In order to span the railroad tracks, the southwest corner was suspended from trusses cantilevered from the vertical piers on its east side. Look up to see the five exposed trusses. The lower 13-story structure contains a parking garage and six floors of computer facilities. The architectural style has an early Modernist influence, especially from the Dutch de Stijl movement. The clock tower is one of the tallest in the world according to the *Guinness Book of World Records*.

Notes

_____

_____

_____

_____

_____

_____

_____

Riverside Plaza Building

(formerly the Chicago Daily News building)

400 W. Madison Street

1929—Holabird and Root, architects

The first building to be erected on railroad air rights, double 12-foot girders were used during construction to cantilever parts of the building over the tracks. It's 26 stories high and has a plaza along the river that was used for band concerts back in the 1930s and is still used today for outdoor events at lunchtime. Its Art Deco design utilizes the concept of the set-back that was popularized in the 1920s and 1930s for more light and ventilation as the area became denser. Because of its innovative engineering and design, the building was awarded the prestigious Architectural League of New York and the American Institute of Architects awards in 1930. It also set the stage for development of the area west of the Chicago River.

Notes

Citicorp Building

(formerly the Northwestern Atrium Building)

500 W. Madison Street

1987—Murphy/Jahn, architects

Designed like a cascading waterfall, this 40-story skyscraper has an arched entrance reminiscent of Louis Sullivan's Transportation and Stock Exchange buildings. The first eight floors form an atrium with retail space. The building also reflects the streamlined Art Deco style of the 1930s and has an exterior skin of thermal glass in blue and reflective silver. The building backs up to the Ogilvie Transportation Center, where Metra trains bring thousands of commuters in and out of downtown daily.

GATEWAY CENTER

A five-building complex, Gateway Center was built on the west bank of the Chicago River over railroad tracks and an area once known as Skid Row. All the buildings, with the exception of 300 S. Riverside Plaza, were designed by Bruce Graham of Skidmore, Owings & Merrill, who also designed the Sears Tower and the John Hancock building. To expedite pedestrian traffic, a people-friendly plaza was added in the 1980s connecting all the buildings.

Notes

10 S. and 120 S. Riverside Plaza

(Gateway I & II)

1965, 1968—Skidmore, Owings & Merrill, architects

These two 20-story, black, steel and glass office buildings make historic reference to the twin, red-brick Butler Brothers buildings designed by Daniel Burnham just to the north of 100 N. Riverside Plaza (the Boeing headquarters). Modernist in design, they exhibit the influence of the Miesian box popular during the 1960s. It should be noted that many of the architects working for Skidmore, Owings & Merrill at this time trained under Mies at the Illinois Institute of Technology and reflected his philosophy of architecture in their building designs. Both buildings are identical. They have a central elevator core with wrap-around floors, tinted windows, and the only architectural ornamentation being the I-beams on the exterior skin of the building.

Notes

_____

_____

_____

_____

_____

_____

222 S. Riverside Plaza

(Gateway III)

1971—Skidmore, Owings & Merrill, architects

This 35-story features the early use of precast panels. These panels made off-site are attached to the steel frame of the building. Precast was a new alternative to steel and glass. The shorter black steel and glass structure with X-braces once housed the Mid-America Commodity Exchange. It now houses a health fitness center.

Notes

_____

_____

_____

_____

_____

_____

_____

_____

_____

_____

300 S. Riverside Plaza

1983—Skidmore, Owings & Merrill, architects

Designed by architect James De Stefano, this is the largest of the buildings in the Gateway complex. It wonderfully exemplifies contextualism in architecture in which the architect adapts the building to the site rather than adapts the site to the building. It contains over one million square feet of space and has a glass curtain wall made up of two sizes of deep green convex glass. As you pass this building on a clear day you can see how the glass panels create a kaleidoscope effect by reflecting the buildings on the east side of the river. It also provides excellent views looking north.

Notes

_____

_____

_____

_____

_____

_____

_____

_____

(Former) Chicago Main Post Office

433 W. Van Buren Street
1921–1933—Graham, Anderson, Probst & White,
architects

With its 2.5 million square feet of space, this huge post office building was the largest in the world when completed in 1931. It was originally part of the 1909 Burnham Plan, which called for a building designed to straddle a major highway. The reason for a post office of this magnitude was to accommodate Chicago's three major catalog houses: Montgomery Ward, Sears and Roebuck, and JC Penney. The building has four towers and a lobby clad in marble with French glass tile reliefs. Multi-storied buildings are not now considered efficient for post offices and therefore a more efficient facility was built to the south. The building has been vacant for a number of years, but recently-announced plans call for a hotel, office building, and condominiums to be part of the site's development.

Notes

(New) U.S. Post Office Central Processing Center

433 W. Harrison Street

1996—Lester B. Knight Architects, Inc.

The new Central Post Office, and its three pavilions for processing and administration, is one of the most automated facilities in the United States. It has green space along the river, though there is no public walkway for security reasons. The building spans the commuter rail lines with ten-foot-deep and 100-foot-long steel I-beams. It has an oversized lobby and service area and a 1,200-car parking garage. There is also a mile-long elevated roadway allowing deliveries by semi-trailers to be made inside the building.

Notes

_____

_____

_____

_____

_____

_____

_____

_____

River City

800 S. Wells Street
1986—Bertrand Goldberg Associates, architects

Originally conceived as four s-shaped buildings that would serpentine down the river, only one structure was built. The 17-story building has 446 apartments (now condominiums), retail and commercial space, a riverfront marina with slips for 70 boats, a health club, and a climate-controlled interior park. The structure is poured concrete and was intended to provide affordable housing and recreational facilities similar to the Marina City complex. The additional three buildings were not approved when density became an issue with the city. The building did, however, help to anchor the redevelopment of the South Loop area, which is one of the hottest real estate development centers in the country.

SOUTH LOOP DEVELOPMENT

Because the city doesn't have any official method of naming neighborhoods, a neighborhood typically earns its name through common usage among residents. In the South Loop, an area just south of downtown, many residents refer to sub areas as Printers Row, Dearborn Park, Near South Loop, Michigan Avenue Historic District, and South Pointe District. The South Loop, along with an area located just west and south of the Field Museum of Natural History campus, has transformed from an industrial and warehouse district to a multi-faceted neighborhood with thousands of new condominiums, conversions, and townhouses.

Notes

Sears Tower

233 S. Wacker Drive
1968–1974, 1985—Skidmore, Owings & Merrill,
architects
1992 renovation and lower-level remodeling—De
Stefano and Partners, architects

For more than 25 years the Sears Tower held the title of the world's tallest building at 110 stories and 1,454 feet. It was designed by Bruce Graham and engineered by Dr. Fazlur Kahn using innovative bundled-tube construction. Nine of these tubes form the base, with the number of tubes reduced with setbacks at the fiftieth, sixty-sixth, and ninetieth floors; twenty-eight acres of black aluminum and bronze-tinted glass windows help create the exterior. The building sits on 114 steel and concrete cassons embedded in bedrock 65 feet below ground, and it can sway 18 inches in all directions to allow for wind shearing, reducing the chances of structural damage. At one time 12,000 employees worked in the building.

In 1985 an atrium was added to the west side to create a friendlier entrance for the routine daily traffic of the Sears Tower; 1994 brought a redesigned entrance for tourists headed to the skydeck. The skydeck boasts 1.5 millions visitors annually, who ascend 1,353 feet in the air for a view that extends to four states on a clear day. Sears moved from the building to Hoffman Estates in the northwest suburbs in 1992, but the building maintained its famous name.

Notes

Chicago Board of Trade

141 W. Jackson Boulevard
1930—Holabird and Root, architects
1980 addition—Murphy/Jahn, Shaw Associates;
Swanke, Hayden, Connell Associates, architects
1997 addition—Fujikawa, Johnson Architects

This Art Deco structure, considered to be one of the finest examples of Art Deco architecture in the city, sits on the site of what was the original Board of Trade Building (designed by W. W. Boyington, who also designed the Chicago Water Tower). Forty-five stories high and clad in gray limestone, the building's pyramidal roof has a 37-foot tall aluminum sculpture by John Storr of Ceres, the Roman goddess of agriculture. For an up close look, see a model in the Art Institute of Chicago. The façade faces north on Jackson Boulevard, looking down LaSalle, Chicago's financial street. Relief sculptures of a hooded figure holding wheat and a Native American holding corn, carved by Illinois sculptor Alvin Meyer, adorn the front. In 1980, architect Helmut Jahn's company added a 12-story steel and reflective glass structure, reminiscent of the original Art Deco building. A huge mural of Ceres by John Warner Norton from the first Board of Trade was reinstalled in the atrium.

Notes

One Financial Place
(The Chicago Stock Exchange)

440 S. LaSalle Street
1985—Skidmore, Owings & Merrill, architects

One Financial Place features 40 bronze-tinted bay windows per floor and is clad in carnelian (red) granite. The corners are chamfered, or cut off, making room for two offices per corner available for lease.

The building has two arched windows reminiscent of Adler and Sullivan's demolished Chicago Stock Exchange Building. The plaza in front of the building has a bronze horse by Ludovico de Luigi which pays homage to the horses atop St. Mark's in Venice.

Notes

_____

_____

_____

_____

_____

_____

_____

_____

_____

Thermal Chicago Corporation Cooling Plant

400 S. Franklin Street
1996—Eckenhoff Saunders, architects

The plant houses the world's largest concrete ice tank, measuring 110 feet by 100 feet by 40 feet. It chills water and returns it for use in air conditioning, and is one of several energy-saving facilities located throughout the Loop area. (In fact, the company operates the world's largest district cooling system and serves nearly 100 buildings downtown.) Its curving, green-glass wall pays homage to the green glass of 333 W. Wacker located at the northern end of Wacker Drive.

Notes

311 S. Wacker Drive

1990—Kohn Pedersen Fox; Harwood K. Smith & Partners, architects

When built, 311 S. Wacker was the tallest concrete-framed building in the world. It is one of three towers originally planned for a block-long site facing South Wacker Drive; the other two were never built due to density concerns. The building is 65 stories and is faced with red granite. An octagonal tower rises from the fifty-first floor and is topped with a glass tower illuminated with 1,400 fluorescent fixtures. The design is held together by a series of bands at the base, thirteenth, and forty-sixth floors.

Notes

_____

_____

_____

_____

_____

_____

_____

_____

_____

200 S. Wacker Drive

1981—Harry Weese & Associates, architects

Composed of two triangles joined at hypotenuses, 200 S. Wacker once again documents Harry Weese's interest in geometric shapes, specifically the triangle. Weese's use of the triangle can also be seen in his River Cottages and the design of the Swissotel. The building's exterior consists of white painted aluminum panels and alternating reflective glass. Weese also designed Quincy Park just south of the building, a pocket park with a 15-foot waterfall and honey locust trees on the site of a razed parking garage.

Notes

Chicago Mercantile Exchange

10 and 30 S. Wacker Drive
1983, 1988—Fujikawa Johnson and Associates,
architects

The two 40-story reinforced-concrete office towers of the Mercantile Exchange are connected at their bases by an 11-story structure that's home to two huge trading floors. The buildings have serrated corners that allow four offices per corner, or sixteen per floor. A covered arcade along the river includes a restaurant and sees live music on summer evenings.

Because the trading floors required a 40,000-square-foot open span without support interruption for trading, it posed quite an engineering problem. The 140-feet by 35-feet trusses would have caused the towers to tilt under their weight, so they were built slightly bowed, and as they were occupied, the curves corrected themselves. The second tower could only be built after the first one was leased. Although they look the same, each tower had to be engineered and designed separately.

Now that the Chicago Board of Trade has merged with the Mercantile Exchange, a move to the Chicago Board of Trade Building is imminent, and the future of the Mercantile Exchange and its huge uninterrupted trading floors is in limbo.

Notes

Civic Opera Building

20 N. Wacker Drive
1929—Graham, Anderson, Probst & White, architects
1996—Skidmore, Owings & Merrill, architects

Real estate and utilities magnate Samuel Insull built the Civic Opera Building as a huge "throne" facing the Chicago River. It is an office building in the Art Deco style with a French Renaissance influence wrapped around a 3,500-seat opera house, home to the Lyric Opera of Chicago. The façade faces Wacker Drive and has a covered walkway or loggia, lavishly decorated with musical motifs, garlands, and comedy and tragedy masks. The 40-foot lobby and interior spaces were created by Jules Guerin, who also designed the lobby's fire curtain. You may remember that we mentioned that Guerin also designed the lobby of the Merchandise Mart.

Completed just before the Great Depression, the building experienced some difficult financial times. Its survival is probably due to the foresight of Samuel Insull, its developer, who included the commercial space for rent. The then-named Chicago Civic Opera House opened on November 4, 1929, with a performance of Verdi's *Aida*.

Notes

_____

_____

_____

_____

110 N. Wacker Drive

1961—Graham, Anderson, Probst & White, architects

This building remains as one of the last reminders of the severe International style of the 1960s. Made of reinforced concrete and sheathed in Indiana limestone, it was once the home of Morton International. The exterior was recently cleaned and enhanced, revealing the presence of fluted stainless panels above and below the paired windows. The building is now outfitted with state of the art technology.

Notes

Great Lakes Building

180 N. Wacker Drive
1912—Holabird & Roche, architects
1983 renovation—Schipporeit Inc., architects

A six-story mill construction building built before Wacker Drive was raised, it was the first building to add green space along the river. It is located on a historic site where a temporary building known as the Wigwam was put up to house the 1860 Republican National Convention. It was in the Wigwam that Abraham Lincoln was nominated to run for president of the United States.

Notes

_____

_____

_____

_____

_____

_____

_____

_____

_____

_____

191 N. Wacker Drive

2002—Kohn, Pedersen Fox Associates; Kendall/Heaton Associates, architects

It is a rare opportunity for a design firm to complete three buildings right next to each other. The last of three buildings designed by the firm of Kohn, Pedersen Fox, it does not compete with its more famous 333 W. Wacker counterpart. The building's lobby cantilevers to the west on the second floor to accommodate the widening of Wacker Drive.

Notes

_____

_____

_____

_____

_____

_____

_____

_____

_____

_____

_____

_____

333 W. Wacker Drive

1983—Kohn, Pedersen Fox Associates; Perkins and Will, architects

A magnificent building on a magnificent site on the bend of the Chicago River, 333 W. Wacker is by far one of the most popular buildings, and perhaps one of the most dramatic, on the Chicago River Architecture Tour. Its glass curtain wall with a 365-foot wide curve is another excellent example of "contextualism": The building responds to the river and reflects the changing sky, buildings, and water. The base of the 36-story building consists of bands of polished dark green marble alternating with gray granite. Because it is so narrow, a diagonal truss system was used to protect the building from wind shearing.

The large circular ventilation ducts are repeated in the firms' other building at 225 W. Wacker Drive. The circular motif has become the company's design signature. The building has won numerous awards and is listed every year as one of Chicago's favorites.

Notes

225 W. Wacker Drive

1989—Kohn, Pedersen Fox Associates; Perkins and Will, architects

Located directly east of 333 W. Wacker, the second building built by Kohn, Pedersen Fox Associates is extremely eclectic, using a variety of materials and design elements. An architectural spire and corner lanterns top the structure; there's an upper-level atrium; and the building's panels under the windows have rivets that reflect its location between two Chicago bridges.

WACKER DRIVE

This double-decked section of Wacker Drive was actually proposed in Burnham's 1909 Plan of Chicago. With upper and lower walkways on the south side and grand staircases leading from the upper level to the street, it was intended to evoke the walkways along the rivers in London and Paris. With the expansion and greening of the city, plans are in place to add a 25-foot floating sidewalk where pedestrians can walk along the river from Michigan Avenue to Wacker Drive. Street vendors and small cafes would enhance the European flavor. Docking of boats would not be allowed. The project is moving along slowly, pending financing.

Notes

222 N. LaSalle Street

1927—Graham, Anderson, Probst & White, architects
1986 remodeling and addition—Skidmore, Owings &
Merrill, architects

Originally planned as a distribution center for the construction trades, this former Builders Building was designed as a steel-framed building clad with glazed brick and terra cotta. The row of triple columns that gives it a look of grandeur was added to what was originally a relatively simple design. The 1986 addition put a four-story glass penthouse on the top. The property to the west was too small to hold a detached building so it was carefully incorporated as an addition with bay windows repeating the window pattern in the main building. During the renovation, the lobby on LaSalle Street was also completely redesigned.

Notes

_____

_____

_____

_____

_____

_____

_____

LaSalle-Wacker Building

221 N. LaSalle Street
1930—Holabird and Root; Rebori, Dewey, Wentworth and McCormick, architects

This building was designed by two wealthy Chicagoans, Joseph Medill Patterson and Robert McCormick, for tenants associated with the banking industry. The 24-story tower designed in an "H" shape was one of the first to utilize setbacks for more light and ventilation when density in the city was becoming an issue.

THE SITE OF THE *EASTLAND* DISASTER

On July 24, 1915, one of the worst maritime disasters occurred at the foot of the Clark Street bridge. Scheduled to take employees from the Western Electric Company on an outing, the *Eastland,* which had a reputation for being unstable, rolled on her side in the river. With more than 2,000 on board, 844 people, most of them young, lost their lives. Twenty-two entire families drowned. The Reid Murdoch Center was turned into a temporary mortuary where desperate family members came to identify their loved ones.

Notes

Waterview Tower

111 W. Wacker Drive

Scheduled for completion, 2009—Teng and Associates, Inc., architects

Under construction at 111 W. Wacker is an 90-story, mixed-use high-rise being built on the site of a former parking lot. The building will house upscale condominiums and the Shangri-La Hotel's first U.S. operation. The hotel will take up floors 12 through 27. Floors 30 through 88 will be residential with a setback at the twenty-ninth floor for a garden. The units will feature one-, two-, and three-bedroom condominiums with floor-to-ceiling bay windows, recessed terraces, marble countertops, and oak-plank flooring.

Notes

_____

_____

_____

_____

_____

_____

_____

77 W. Wacker

(formerly known as the R. R Donnelley building)

1992—Ricardo Bofill Arquitectura, De Stefano and
Partners, architects

Meant to represent a giant column similar to Giotto's campanile
(bell tower) on the Florence, Italy, cathedral, this excellent
example of Post-modernism is actually categorized as Modern
Classicism. Ricardo Bofill wanted to merge the glass of
modernism with the classical element of stone. The lobby has
dramatic light fixtures and a sculpture by Xavier Corbero. The
base is 42 feet high, and the top is capped with classical
pediments similar to Greek temple architecture. The building is
handsomely illuminated at night.

Notes

_____

_____

_____

_____

_____

_____

_____

Leo Burnett Building

35 W. Wacker Drive

1989—Kevin Roche and John Dinkeloo and Associates, architects

Home of one of the world's largest advertising agencies, 35 W. Wacker has 50 stories of reinforced concrete and was designed as a column within a column. The weight of the building is redistributed from the exterior walls to the interior columns, allowing for wrap-around, non-weight-bearing windows. The exterior is polished gray granite and has stainless steel mullions that change with the light of day. The building conforms to Louis Sullivan's classic definition: a clearly defined base, shaft, and capital. Architect Kevin Roche was awarded the Pritzker Prize for Architecture in 1984.

Notes

_____

_____

_____

_____

_____

_____

_____

35 E. Wacker Drive

(formerly the Jewelers building, then the Pure Oil building)

1926—Glaver & Dinkelberg, Thielbar & Fugard, architects

The design of 35 E. Wacker is based on a fifteenth-century Italian monastery. Its elaborately decorated exterior may have been considered appropriate for the original occupants of the building— jewelry designers and retailers. With a skin of terra cotta, it has a 24-story base and a 17-story tower capped with a belvedere that offers spectacular views of the city. A twenty-fourth floor terrace was eliminated for reasons of security. Because the building had adequate light, an automobile elevator was added to the central core. This provided extra safety for jewelers carrying precious stones into the building. The elevator was abandoned around 1940 due to mechanical problems. The belvedere at the top of the building once housed the Stratosphere Lounge frequented by gangster Al Capone. Today that space is part of the offices of the architecture firm of Murphy/Jahn.

Notes

75 E. Wacker Drive

(also known as the Lincoln Tower and Mather Tower)

1928—Hubert Hugh Riddle, architect

Once known as the skinniest skyscraper in Chicago, this 42-story building is topped with an 18-story tower. The forty-second floor is only nine feet, six inches across and the thirty-ninth-floor office space is only 250 square feet. A second building was to be built with the two joined at the base, but the Depression eliminated any hope of that happening. Recently, four of the top floors were removed because they were structurally unsound. The cupola was taken down and stored on a barge on the river while the removal took place and then was hoisted back on top by helicopters. The original developer was Alonzo Mather, who made his money when he invented a train car for the humane transport of animals.

Notes

_____

_____

_____

_____

_____

_____

_____

360 N. Michigan Avenue

(Also known as the London Guarantee and Accident
Building and the Stone Container Building)

1922, 1923—Alfred S. Alschuler, architect

Just opposite the Wrigley Building and on the site of Fort
Dearborn, the 22-story Indiana limestone building is filled with
classical Greco-Roman influences and is topped with a tempietto.
Its ornamentation is consistent with the Beaux Arts tradition of
borrowing from other architecture styles. The griffins and coats of
arms from London that grace the lobby are reminders that the
building was originally known as the London Guarantee Building.
The famous London House, with headline performers like Frank
Sinatra and Sammy Davis Jr., was also once at this address. It is
now sometimes called the Crain Communications Building for its
prominent tenant.

Notes

333 N. Michigan Avenue

1928—Holabird & Root, architects

Based on Eero Saarinen's second-prize design for the Tribune Competition, 333 N. Michigan was Chicago's first Art Deco building and the last of the four buildings to complete the gateway between the Chicago Loop and north Michigan Avenue. It has a polished marble base and huge seven-foot panels, designed by Fred Torrey, documenting the early history of Chicago.

Notes

One Illinois Center

111 E. Wacker Drive
1971—Mies van der Rohe, architect

Two Illinois Center

233 N. Michigan Avenue
1973—Office of Mies van der Rohe, architects

Three Illinois Center

303 E. Wacker Drive
1980—Fujikawa Conterato Lohan & Associates,
architects

Begun in 1967, this development spreads over 80 acres of obsolete railroad yards. The first building completed was One Illinois Center, a 30-story black glass and steel office building. Following Mies's death, his successor firm of Fujikawa Conterato Lohan & Associates continued designing Two and Three Illinois Center. The stark Modernist style did nothing to enhance the surroundings. A colorful sculpture, "Splash" by Jerry Peart, was installed in 1986 to add color and life to the area. There is an underground walkway connecting the buildings that seems to have struggled with retail success.

Notes

Two Prudential Plaza

180 N. Stetson Avenue

1990—Loebl, Schlossman & Hackl, architects

One Prudential Plaza

130 E. Randolph Street

1955—Naess & Murphy, architects

Although we don't get a proper view of this 63-story building, if you look between the towers of the Hyatt Regency Hotel you will at least see it. At 920 feet high, when it was built it was the second tallest reinforced-concrete building in the city. It closely resembles a design by Helmut Jahn in Philadelphia called Liberty Place. The building has chevron-shaped setbacks with a diamond-faceted apex.

The original Prudential Building can be seen to the west, although the view is also limited. To truly see the old Prudential Building I suggest you go to Millennium Park. The old Prudential Building was the tallest building in Chicago in 1955.

The chevron motif at Two Prudential Plaza is repeated in the entranceways. At night the apex is illuminated with 230 exterior lights positioned in its setbacks. The complex also features a one-acre Beaubien Plaza named for the city's first innkeeper. It is graced with waterfalls and terraces and shielded from the sun by the original building.

Notes

Hyatt Regency Hotel

151 E. and 171 E. Wacker Drive.
1974–80—A. Epstein & Sons, architects

These two brown-brick buildings hold 2,051 rooms, making it the largest hotel in the Hyatt chain. It's also the largest hotel in Chicago and boasts an enormous ballroom, extensive convention facilities, and a 4,000-square-foot lagoon in its lobby.

Notes

_____

_____

_____

_____

_____

_____

_____

_____

_____

_____

_____

Swissotel Chicago

323 E. Wacker Drive

1989—Harry Weese and Associates, architects

Located at the eastern edge of Illinois Center, the Swissotel features 624 luxury rooms. The building's design forms two equilateral triangles, sheathed in alternating bands of silver-tinted opaque and reflective glass, that creates space around the perimeter for windows eliminating long corridors and the institutional look.

Notes

_____

_____

_____

_____

_____

_____

_____

_____

_____

_____

Lake Shore East Development

LAKESHORE EAST: THE LANCASTER

201 N. Westshore Drive
2004—Loewenberg Architects

LAKESHORE EAST: THE SHOREHAM

400 E. South Water Street
2005—Loewenberg Architects

LAKESHORE EAST: THE REGATTA

420 E. Waterside Drive
2006—De Stefano and Partners, architects

LAKESHORE EAST: AQUA

225 N. Columbus Drive
Scheduled for completion, 2009—Studio Gang
Architects

When completed, this development will have between 10 to 12 high-rise condominium buildings, townhouses, retail space, and a park. One of the high-rises currently under construction is the Aqua designed by Jean Gang's Studio Gang Architects. Aqua will rise 84 stories and feature an undulating glass curtain wall that will appear like ripples in the water. It is estimated Lake Shore East will add 12,000 people to residential life along the river.

Notes

Aon Center

(formerly Amoco and Standard Oil buildings)

200 E. Randolph Street

1972—Edward Durell Stone and Perkins & Will, architects

The second-tallest building in Chicago, at 80 stories and 1,136 feet, Aon Center had an original skin of white Italian marble, which became a liability when it began to pull away from the building. Although nothing ever fell, the entire building had to be re-clad with granite from North Carolina at an estimated cost of between $60 and $80 million. Something unique about this structure is that the mechanicals run up the corners of the building eliminating any mechanical floors as part of the design. The owners recently announced that the top ten floors may be turned into condominiums.

Notes

THE CHICAGO LOCK

Built by the Army Corps of Engineers in 1937, the locks are 600 feet long and 80 feet wide and provide major access from the Chicago River to Lake Michigan. The locks were added after the reversal of the Chicago River when it was determined that an unusual amount of Lake Michigan water was flowing west into the river.

The locks operate 24 hours a day. There is no lock fee, but there is priority usage. Emergency vessels such as those of the Chicago Police Department's marine division and the United States Coast Guard take precedence. They are followed by tour boats like those you experienced at Wendella, then commercial traffic, and finally pleasure craft. It is reported that more than 42,000 vessels pass through the locks each year.

REVERSAL OF THE CHICAGO RIVER

After numerous water-related deaths were reported as caused by polluted Lake Michigan water, early city planners decided that the only way to resolve the problem was to reverse the flow of the Chicago River. The plan called for a 28-mile-long canal to connect the Chicago and Des Plaines rivers. The canal would be dredged 15 feet deeper than the river and, when opened, gravity would pull the river backwards naturally. On January 2, 1900, the project was completed, the canal opened, and the Chicago River has flowed west, opposite its original course, ever since. The result: clean drinking water for Chicago and over 150 communities around Chicago that depend on Lake Michigan for their drinking-water supply.

Navy Pier

1916—Charles S. Frost, architect
1976 ballroom restoration—Jerome R. Butler, architect
1990s work—Benjamin Thompson & Associates, architects; VOA Associates, architects

Originally called Municipal Pier, Navy Pier was built in 1916 and was an important terminal for freight and passenger traffic from 1918 through 1930. At one point it was used to train naval personnel for the war effort. Between 1946 and 1965 it was home to the Chicago branch of the University of Illinois. In 1993, a $150 million reconstruction project began to turn the pier into an exposition and entertainment center. Today the pier includes an IMAX theater, children's museum, stained glass museum, Shakespeare theater, 1,500-seat outdoor theater, shops and restaurants, and the renovated Festival Hall, which is still used for major events. It is now listed as one of the major tourist attractions in Illinois. Plans are underway to expand Navy Pier even further to attract more visitors during the winter months.

Notes

Lake Point Tower Condominiums

505 N. Lake Shore Drive
1968—George Schipporeit and John Heinrich,
architects, with Graham, Anderson, Probst & White

Based on an original design of Mies van der Rohe for a 30-story office building in Berlin that never materialized, Lake Point Tower was designed by two of Mies's students in tribute to the master teacher. When it was completed in 1968, its 70 stories made it the tallest apartment building in the world. Its bronze-tinted glass curtain wall wraps an undulating design built to handle strong winds off Lake Michigan. Students from the University of Wisconsin installed instruments for measuring the impact of the wind on the building. It is the only building built east of Lake Shore Drive on landfill. It has a three-acre park with a swimming pool at the base, and a restaurant tenant in the circular top. The original 823 apartments have been converted to condominiums.

Notes

Proposed Site of the Chicago Spire

400 N. Lake Shore Drive
Scheduled for completion, 2010—Santiago Calatrava,
architect, with Perkins and Will

Approved by the Chicago City Council in 2007, the 150-story,
2000-foot Chicago Spire will top out as the tallest building in the
country and the tallest residential building (condominiums) in the
world. The building design has been compared to a drill bit; the
twisting allows for structural integrity against stormy winds off
Lake Michigan. A community room is planned at the top that will
offer views of four states.

Notes

Riverview I and II

445 E. Water Street

2001, 2006—DeStefano and Partners, architects

A two-phase complex, Riverview is comprised of a 32-story west tower and a 29-story east tower with town homes surrounding the base. The buildings have a steel cornice and are well-designed in comparison with their neighbors. The complex includes indoor and outdoor swimming pools, a park, a health club, a promenade along the river, and spectacular views.

Notes

_____

_____

_____

_____

_____

_____

_____

_____

_____

_____

Nicholas J. Melas Centennial Fountain

McClurg Court at the Chicago River
1989—Lohan Associates

Designed by the grandson of Mies van der Rohe, the fountain honors the Metropolitan Water Reclamation District, the agency charged with ensuring that we have a constant supply of good water in Chicago. The water on the east side that cascades down represents the Great Lakes as it passes through the St. Lawrence Seaway and the Atlantic Ocean. The water on the west side symbolizes the path through the Chicago, Des Plaines, and Illinois rivers to the Mississippi River and Gulf of Mexico. The large round disk represents the Continental Divide. The fountain has a water cannon that shoots a stream of water 90 feet into the air the first ten minutes of each hour in the late spring and summer seasons. The cannon is designed so that boats can pass underneath; however, due to gravity, not without getting their passengers wet.

Notes

Sheraton Center Hotel

301 N. Water Street
1992—Solomon, Cordwell, and Buenz & Associates,
architects

Currently the fourth largest hotel in Chicago, it has 1,200 rooms, more than 120,000 square feet of meeting space, and a banquet facility the size of a football field that will hold 5,000 people. The tower section offers upgraded accommodations and services on four private floors, including butler service, afternoon tea, complimentary breakfast, and hors d'oeuvres. The green glass windows in the hotel reflect the color of the Chicago River. It also boasts a wonderful promenade with spectacular views of the river and the city.

Notes

NBC Tower

454 N. Columbus Drive
1989—Skidmore, Owings & Merrill, architects

The production facility of NBC's Channel 5, the building pays homage to Raymond Hood's RCA Tower, a centerpiece of the Rockefeller Center in New York City. A contemporary interpretation of Art Deco, it features setback design and flying buttresses on the north and south ends as a nod to the Tribune Tower, its neighbor to the west. Its architectural spire is 127 feet tall and the dark panels under the windows add to the vertical feeling. A four-story production facility is attached on the north side.

Notes

_____

_____

_____

_____

_____

_____

_____

_____

John Hancock Building

875 N. Michigan Avenue

1969—Skidmore, Owings & Merrill, architects

The John Hancock Building has anchored North Michigan Avenue since it was completed in 1969. It's the third-tallest building in Chicago at 1127 feet and 100 stories, and it boasts 2.8 million square feet of residential and commercial space. The ingenious cross-bracing, an engineering design by Dr. Fazlur Kahn, who also worked on the Sears Tower, was created to help the building become more resistant to the wind. The observatory on the ninety-fifth floor is open to the public with spectacular views of the city and lake. Although you do not get a good look at the building from the river, we suggest that you take a walk north on Michigan Avenue and experience the building firsthand.

Notes

_____

_____

_____

_____

_____

_____

_____

_____

University of Chicago Gleacher Center

450 N. Cityfront Plaza Drive
1993—Lohan Associates, architects

Built as a downtown facility for the University of Chicago, the Gleacher Center has 27 classrooms located on the west side of the building. Criticized for its lack of windows in the classrooms given its spectacular location, architect Dirk Lohan, the grandson of Mies van der Rohe, countered that this was his way of not distracting students.

Notes

Equitable Building

401 N. Michigan Avenue

1965—Skidmore, Owings & Merrill, architects

When the Equitable Building was built the height and setback were established by the Tribune Company, which owned the land. The site is very near where the trading cabin of Jean Baptist Pointe du Sable, Chicago's first non-Native American resident, sat. It also is close to the original site of the reaper factory of Cyrus Hall McCormick that opened in 1847. The 35-story building is typical of the Modernist designs of the 1960s and features bronze-tinted aluminum windows.

Notes

_____

_____

_____

_____

_____

_____

_____

_____

Tribune Tower

435 N. Michigan Avenue
1925—Raymond Hood and John Mead Howells,
architects

In 1922, the *Chicago Tribune* held an international competition to select a design for their new building. The firm of Hood and Howells was chosen from more than 250 entries. The building's exterior is Indiana limestone. The Neo-Gothic design was inspired by the Rouen Cathedral in France, the Cathedral of Malines in Belgium, and the popular Woolworth Building in New York City by Cass Gilbert. Although considered retro at the time, it has endeared itself to Chicagoans over the years and has become a local favorite. Stones from all over the world are embedded in the exterior, including a piece from the Parthenon, the pyramids, and even the moon. The three-story, arched entryway contains a screen filled with characters from Aesop's fables.

Notes

CONCLUSION

In 1906, Daniel H. Burnham and his assistant Edward H. Bennett backed by the Merchants' and Commercial clubs, initiated a master Plan of Chicago. The plan was finalized in 1909 and presented a blueprint for how public spaces could be transformed into grandiose areas reminiscent of Beaux Arts Paris.

The lakefront was set aside for recreation and Grant Park and the Monroe Harbor would be the "front door" to the city. The Commercial Club established the Chicago Plan Commission that eventually led to the first comprehensive zoning laws for the city. In 1920, the opening of the Michigan Avenue bridge pushed the development north of the river.

The Chicago River today has motivated new growth and extensive revitalization. Recent architectural additions, along with a master plan for development along the river, have taken Burnham's Plan into the twenty-first century, encouraging pedestrian and environmentally-friendly promenades and green space.

Today, the river is a showcase for some of the great architecture of the world, a visual reminder of what we can accomplish in our environment. We reversed it first in 1900 when it was so badly polluted it actually had a negative effect on our physical well-being. In a sense, we have reversed it once again a century later, in transforming an industrialized, dirty, "working" river into a centerpiece waterway that lifts our spirits and inspires us with its natural and constructed grandeur.

Other Things to Do on Michigan Avenue

Now that you have taken The Chicago River Architecture Tour, you may be looking for other things to do within walking distance of the Wrigley Building. Here are a few suggestions:

TRIBUNE TOWER

435 N. Michigan Avenue
Just across the street from the Wrigley Building, this is the home of the *Chicago Tribune* and the WGN radio studios. You can watch through a glass window the news being broadcast live.

FREEDOM MUSEUM

435 N. Michigan Avenue
A new Chicago museum devoted to the freedoms of the First Amendment, located in the Tribune building. It offers 45-minute tours Monday through Friday.

BILLY GOAT TAVERN

Lower Michigan Avenue at E. Hubbard Street.
Made famous with John Belushi's "cheezboogga" skit on TV's *Saturday Night Live* and the Chicago Cubs curse, this lively spot is a longtime hangout for journalists. (There is a staircase from upper Michigan Avenue that you can descend to the underground entrance. Just look for the sign.)

MUSEUM OF CONTEMPORARY ART

220 E. Chicago Avenue
Dedicated to the avant-garde, this art-world institution has been in this new location since 1996. Designed by Berlin architect Josef Paul Kleihues, it holds 220,000 square feet of exhibit space, a wonderful terrace overlooking a sculpture garden, and a terrific gift shop.

JOHN HANCOCK CENTER

875 N. Michigan Avenue
Just walk north four blocks on Michigan Avenue and you will be standing in front of "Big John." Finished in 1969, this was the tallest building in the world until the Sears Tower came along. There is an observatory on the 94th floor with spectacular views of the lake and the city. Need some liquid refreshment or food? Stop at the Images Lounge on the ninety-sixth floor or the upscale Signature Room on the ninety-fifth floor. Both offer great views of the city panorama.

CHICAGO WATER TOWER

800 N. Michigan Avenue
Designed in 1869, this structure by one of Chicago's first architects, W. W. Boyington, survived the Great Chicago Fire of 1871. The grassy area surrounding it is a great place to sit and people watch.

CARRIAGE RIDES

Horse-drawn carriages with their top-hatted drivers can take you on a narrated tour. The carriages are at Pearson Street and Michigan Avenue just outside the Chicago Water Tower.

SHOPPING ON THE MAGNIFICENT MILE

Shop until you drop. Here's a strip to buy anything your heart desires. Don't be fooled into thinking that the only stores are the ones you can see. Several of the buildings include seven or eight floors of additional shops. Among them are:

WATER TOWER PLACE

835 N. Michigan Avenue
Seven stories of shops, restaurants, and movie theaters.

900 N. MICHIGAN AVENUE

Eight retail floors anchored by Bloomingdale's.

CHICAGO PLACE

700 N. Michigan Avenue
Eight retail floors, including Saks Fifth Avenue, Talbot's, and Ann Taylor.

Other establishments include Tiffany's, Neiman Marcus, Banana Republic, and Crate and Barrel. Just walk north along Michigan Avenue and you can window shop (or the real deal) for hours.

If you walk south on Michigan Avenue and cross the Michigan Avenue bridge, you might want to visit:

THE ART INSTITUTE OF CHICAGO

Michigan Avenue at Adams Street
One of the foremost art museums in the world, our art museum has the second-largest collection of Impressionist paintings in the world. It also has art from around the world and a wonderful collection of works by American artists. Note the two lions guarding the museum by sculptor Edward Kemeys. The building was originally built to house the Congress that preceded the World's Columbian Exposition of 1893.

CHICAGO CULTURAL CENTER

78 E. Washington Street at Michigan Avenue
The original main branch of the Chicago Public Library, the Cultural Center is now home base for a variety of exhibits and cultural offerings. Be sure to walk up the stairs to see magnificent Preston Bradley Hall topped with an illuminated stained-glass dome by Louis Comfort Tiffany.

MILLENNIUM PARK

Michigan Avenue between Washington and Monroe streets
Originally conceived to open with the turn of the millennium, Chicago's newest showpiece park opened a few years past 2000, but became an instant local hit and international sensation. Its 23 acres feature an outdoor concert area with enclosed orchestra platform designed by famed architect Frank Gehry. It also features a popular sculpture piece by Anish Kapoor, "Cloudgate," but affectionately re-dubbed "the Bean." Be sure to see the Crown Fountain by Jaume Plensa, which is an interactive fountain featuring LED screens showing the faces of more than 1,000 Chicago residents. And by all means check out the Lurie Garden, a tribute to Chicago's motto "Urbs in Horto" or "City in a Garden." Here you can see more than 138 varieties of perennial plants and flowering cherry trees.

SUGGESTED READING
CHICAGO ARCHITECTURE

Badger, Reid. *The Great American Fair: The World's Columbian Exposition & American Culture*. Chicago: Nelson Hall, 1979.

Condit, Carl W. *The Chicago School of Architecture*. Chicago and London: The University of Chicago Press, 1964.

Drexler, Arthur. *Ludwig Mies van der Rohe*. London: Mayflower Publishing Company; New York: George Braziller, Inc., 1960.

Heise, Kenan. *Chicago: The Beautiful*. Chicago: Bonus Books, Inc. 2001.

Hines, Thomas S. *Burnham of Chicago: Architect and Planner*. Chicago: The University of Chicago Press, 1979.

O'Gorman, Thomas J. *Architecture in Detail Chicago*. New York: Sterling Publishing Co., Inc. 2003.

Pridmore, Jay and Larson, George A. *Chicago Architecture and Design*. New York: Harry N. Abrams, Inc., 2005.

Schulze, Franz. *Mies van der Rohe: A Critical Biography*. Chicago: University of Chicago Press, 1985.

Schulze, Franz and Harrington, Kevin. *Chicago's Famous Buildings*, 5th Edition. Chicago: The University of Chicago Press, 2003.

Sinkevitch, Alice, Editor. *AIA Guide to Chicago*, 2nd Edition. New York: Harcourt, Inc., 2004.

Zukowsky, John and Thorne, Martha. *Masterpieces of Chicago Architecture*. New York: Rizzoli International Publications, Inc., 2004.

Zukowsky, John, Editor. *Chicago Architecture 1872–1922, Birth of a Metropolis*. Munich: Prestel-Verlag Publishers, 1987.

Zukowsky, John. Editor. *Chicago Architecture and Design: 1923–1993*. Munich: Prestel-Verlag Publishers, 1993.

Uhl, Michael. *Frommer's Walking Tours: Chicago*. New York: Prentice Hall Travel, 1994.

CHICAGO RIVER

Hill, Libby. *The Chicago River: A Natural and Unnatural History*. Chicago: Lake Claremont Press, 2000.

Solzman, David M. *The Chicago River: An Illustrated History and Guide to the River and Its Waterways.* Chicago: Loyola Press, 1998.

CHICAGO HISTORY

Cutler, Irving. *Chicago: Metropolis of the Mid-Continent,* 3rd Edition. Dubuque, Iowa: Kendall/Hunt Publishing Company, 1982.

Danckers, Ulrich and Meredith, Jane. *Early Chicago.* River Forest, Ill.: Early Chicago, Inc., 2000.

Gilbert. James. *Perfect Cities: Chicago's Utopias of 1893.* Chicago: University of Chicago Press, 1991.

Heise, Kenan and Frazel, Mark. *Hands on Chicago: Getting Hold of the City.* Chicago: Bonus Books, Inc., 1987.

Mayer, Harold M. and Wade, Richard C. *Chicago: Growth of A Metropolis.* Chicago: The University of Chicago Press, 1969.

Miller, Donald L. *City of the Century.* New York: Simon & Schuster, 1996.

Spinney, Robert G. *City of Big Shoulders: A History of Chicago.* De Kalb, Illinois: Northern Illinois Press, 2000.

INDEX

Publisher's Credits

Cover design by Timothy Kocher. Interior design and layout by Todd Petersen. Pocket by Charisse Antonopoulos. Editing by Bruce Clorfene, Diana Solomon and Sharon Woodhouse. Index by June Sawyer.

Note

Although Lake Claremont Press and the author, editors, and others affiliated with *The Chicago River Architecture Tour* have exhaustively researched all sources to ensure the accuracy and completeness of the information contained within this book, we assume no responsibility for errors, inaccuracies, omissions, or inconsistencies herein.

Acknowledgments

I would personally like to thank Michael Borgstrom, President of Wendella Boats, for his encouragement and support in bringing this project to closure, and to the Borgstrom family for sharing details of their family history and the evolution of their company. Special thanks to Robert Borgstrom for sharing his stories of Wendella's early years, and to Steve Borgstrom for sharing his fond memories of growing up in the family business.

In addition, I would like to thank Sharon Woodhouse of Lake Claremont Press for her patience and professional guidance throughout this project, and lisa scacco, LCP Production Manager, for pulling the project together.

For his inspiration and encouragement, thanks to Rick Kogan, feature writer with the *Chicago Tribune.*

Thanks to my colleagues at Wendella Boats, Craig F. Wenokur and Jennifer M. Perry, for allowing me to use many of their wonderful photographs taken on the river, and to Gregg E. Pupecki for his ongoing technical assistance.

A special thank you to my sister, Evelyn, for her support and patience.

To the designers, Timothy Kocher (cover) and Todd Petersen (interior), who took the photographs and copy and created a visually attractive document.

And finally, to all the people who have taken my Chicago River Architecture Tour over the last 22 years and have encouraged me to put pen to paper.

Photo Credits

The Borgstrom family, Glen Carpenter, Craig F. Wenokur, Jennifer M. Perry, Robert De Caprio, Jr., Image Fiction, Gary Cooper, Cooper Communications, Inc., Chicago Public Library, Special Collections and Preservation Division, and Teng & Associates, Architects. Waterview Tower rendering compliments of Teng & Associates, Architects.

About the Author

Phyllis J. Kozlowski, Ph.D., is a native Chicagoan who grew up in the Back of the Yards neighborhood. She has always had a passion for the city and its architecture, and has lectured and escorted tour groups for years. For more than 20 years, she has led groups on Chicago River architecture tours for the Chicago Architecture Foundation and for a number of tour companies that operate boats on the Chicago River and Lake Michigan. In addition to escorting local groups, she has accompanied tours to more than 35 countries.

Retired as Chairman of the Fine Arts and Humanities Department at Moraine Valley Community College, she is currently the Director of Education and Guest Services at Wendella Boats, which has been providing tours on the lake and river since 1935.

With a Ph.D. from the Ohio State University in art education, Dr. Kozlowski continues to serve as an adjunct faculty member in DePaul University's School for New Learning, where she teaches a course called "Chicago: Emergence of a Metropolis," and at Elmhurst College, where she teaches art and architecture history. When not giving tours of Chicago, she exhibits as a watercolorist and continues to travel extensively.

Lake Claremont Press

Founded in 1994, Lake Claremont Press specializes in books on the Chicago area and its history, focusing on preserving the city's past, exploring its present environment, and cultivating a strong sense of place for the future. Visit us on the Web at *www.lakeclaremont.com*.

SELECTED BOOKLIST

From Lumber Hookers to the Hooligan Fleet: A Treasury of Chicago Maritime History

Finding Your Chicago Irish

Today's Chicago Blues

Chicago TV Horror Movie Shows: From Shock Theatre to Svengoolie

The Golden Age of Chicago Children's Television

Graveyards of Chicago

Oldest Chicago

The SportsTraveler's Fanbook to Chicago

Wrigley Field's Last World Series

A Chicago Tavern: A Goat, a Curse, and the American Dream

Great Chicago Fires

A Native's Guide to Chicago

For Members Only: A History and Guide to Chicago's Oldest Private Clubs

I Am a Teamster: A Short, Fiery Story of Regina V. Polk, Her Hats, Her Pets, Sweet Love, and the Modern-Day Labor Movement

Rule 53: Capturing Hippies, Spies, Politicians, and Murderers in an American Courtroom

AWARD-WINNERS

The Chicago River: A Natural and Unnatural History

The Politics of Place: A History of Zoning in Chicago

Finding Your Chicago Ancestors

The Streets & San Man's Guide to Chicago Eats

A Cook's Guide to Chicago

Notes

Notes

Notes

Notes